DON'T QUIT

UNTIL YOU TASTE THE

Honey

Encouragement for
STRESSED-OUT
CHRISTIANS

W. GLYN EVANS

BROADMAN PRESS
NASHVILLE, TENNESSEE

4260-66
ISBN: 0-8054-6066-7

Dewey Decimal Classification: 248.4
Subject Heading: CHRISTIAN LIFE // DEVOTIONAL LITERATURE
Library of Congress Card Catalog Number: 92-24791
Printed in the United States of America

Unless otherwise noted, all Scripture quotations are from the Holy Bible, *New International Version,* copyright © 1973, 1978, 1984 by International Bible Society.

Scripture quotations marked KJV are from the *King James Version* of the Bible.

Scripture quotations marked RSV are from the *Revised Standard Version of the Bible,* copyrighted 1946, 1952, © 1971, 1973 by the National Council of the Churches of Christ in the U.S.A., and used by permission.

Scripture quotations marked NKJV are from the *New King James Version.* Copyright © 1979, 1980, 1982, Thomas Nelson, Inc., Publishers.

Library of Congress Cataloging-in-Publication Data

Evans, W. Glyn (William Glyn)
    Don't quit until you taste the honey / W. Glyn Evans.
      p.   cm.
    ISBN 0-8054-6066-7
    1. Stress (Psychology)—Religious aspects—Christianity—Meditations. 2. Peace of mind—Religious aspects—Christianity—Meditations. I. Title.
BV4501.2.E89   1993
242—dc20   92-24791
                                              CIP

To all the congregations
it has been our privilege to serve,
who have proved the truth
of Jesus' statement:

"You are the salt of the earth."

Introduction

I have long since forgotten many of the chapel messages I heard in my years of undergraduate study at Wheaton (Ill.) College. But one message, delivered twice a year by President V. Raymond Edman, will remain with me always. It was entitled "It's Always Too Soon to Quit" and was timed for the weary period of college life, usually near the end of each semester. The message was a booster, a tonic, a shot in the arm. Edman would describe inventors like Ford and Edison, who performed hundreds of experiments before they finally triumphed in creating cars and incandescent lights. What if they had quit too soon? So Edman went on, showing the value of sticking to it, waiting it out and, finally, triumphing!

Well, in one way or another, my message to God's people during forty years of pastoring has been the same. Don't quit, victory lies ahead! Isn't this what Paul said to Archippus? "See to it that you complete the work you have received in the Lord" (Col. 4:17). I don't know what Archippus' problem was, but the solution Paul recommends to him makes me feel that he was on the point of throwing in the towel. And when I look around at the morale level of God's people today, I believe that many are afflicted with the "I've had it!" feeling.

That's where Don't Quit Until You Taste the Honey comes in. Beginning with the story of Samson and the lion, I have offered messages of encouragement and hope. My aim has been to edify. I have concentrated on the available resources of God to meet every need. It is a "feel-good" book, but based upon spiritual reality, not naiveté. Time and again I have found God's resources to be adequate, even abundant, for my own needs. Out of this background I have stretched out my hand to help brothers and sisters in Christ who have reached the stress point in the service of the Lord.

I've arranged the messages in short, one-page "bursts" to make them more readily usable than if they were couched in long chapters. As minute doses, they can be read each day as companions to your devotional time with the Lord. Sometimes they can be expanded into a larger personal Bible study, in which you can explore some of the Bible verses suggested and record your own personal thoughts as the Lord directs you. Or the material can be incorporated into your teaching or preaching ministry. Also, the pages can be used in small group Bible study for discussion and application. At family prayer time they can be read, discussed, and applied as the need dictates. In personal, one-on-one discipleship, they can be the basis of exhortation and instruction.

In my earlier days of ministry, one of my favorite authors was Frank W. Boreham. In one of his books he tells of Allan Gillespie, the pastor of a small country church high in the hills of New Zealand. Allan became discouraged with his church. He felt they were not responsive to the gospel. He decided it was time for him to quit. He moved to a town in the valley below and took up other work. Some time after he left, a revival broke out in the church and all that Allan had hoped for came to pass. But he was not there to enjoy it; he had quit too soon.

For all of us who serve the Lord, there is the temptation to quit too soon. No doubt that's why the writer to the Hebrews encouraged his readers: "So do not throw away your confidence; it will be richly rewarded. You need to persevere so that when you have done the will of God, you will receive what he has promised" (Heb. 10:35-36).

That's what I've tried to say in this book.

Don't Quit
Until You Taste the Honey

Samson, the Bible strong man, met a young lion on his way to the Philistine town of Timnah (Judg. 14:5). The lion roared defiance, but Samson seized the animal and "he tore the lion apart with his bare hands" (v. 6). Later, he returned to Timnah and looked around to see what happened to the lion's carcass. He found that bees had hived inside the lion and left a large residue of honey. He scooped out the honey and devoured it.

There's a lesson here for us all. When we meet lions of one kind or another, we take them to be signs of God's *disfavor* instead of an opportunity to taste God's *victory*. How many times have we quit too soon?

Look at the pattern Jesus left us. What a "lion" He faced at Calvary! But He suffered long enough to make His death yield the honey of resurrection; He "endured" the cross because of the "joy set before him" (Heb. 12:2).

Every trial we face carries in it the seeds of a wonderful victory. If we cling to His will and lean on His arm, those seeds will sprout, blossom, and bear fruit to our wonder and joy. On the other hand, if we avoid the problem, cut our losses, and back off too soon, we're not giving God enough time to create the honey of victory.

At the end of his Letter to the Colossians, Paul wrote: "Tell Archippus, 'See to it that you complete the work you have received in the Lord'" (Col. 4:17). What was Archippus' problem? No one knows. Whatever it was, the apostle didn't want his friend to quit before he tasted the honey. Paraphrased, Paul might have said: "Don't cave in to your problem until it yields the victory God intends for you to have."

It's always too soon to quit before you taste the honey.

Do not throw away your confidence; it will be richly rewarded.
You need to persevere so that when you have done the will
of God, you will receive what he has promised
(Heb. 10:35-36).

Building a Friendship with God

God invites us to build a friendship with Him. Friendship is a relationship, and relationships are built upon an agreed set of conditions. God can invite us to be His friends only if we agree. "Can two walk together, except they be agreed?" (Amos 3:3, KJV). This means more than having similar thoughts; it means coming up to the conditions which make friendship with God possible.

One thing He requires is that we remove anything in our lives that is offensive to Him. Friendship cannot survive offensiveness. When Jesus washed the disciples' feet, He established the condition of friendship with them—cleanliness. After the washing, He called them His friends (John 15:15), but He reminded them that if they wanted to continue the friendship, they had to live according to His standard: "You are my friends if you do what I command" (v. 14).

Our greatest hindrance in being a friend of God is being unwilling to acknowledge the smudges on our faces. He is patient with all of our weaknesses, except the desire to excuse our sins. Our friendship with Him must be secured by the cleansing power of Christ's blood. If we deal honestly with our smudges, all He promised in Hosea 14 will be ours: lily beauty, cedar fragrance, vine fruit, and pine greenness. Friendships are cherished by God, and no one who walks with Him will lose.

We need not worry about God fulfilling His side of the bargain. He not only fills it, He overflows it. He walks with His friends in close confidentiality. "The Lord confides in those who fear him; he makes his covenant known to them" (Ps. 25:14). Jesus said that although servants are not privy to the Master's secrets, friends are (John 15:15). This means that friendship with God is an unspeakable privilege, and privilege means learning the ways of His heart.

The Lord would speak to Moses face to face, as a man speaks with his friend (Ex. 33:11).

Renewed!

Who is the creative agent of God? The Holy Spirit! He is a renewing Spirit; He renews the *earth* (Gen. 1:2), and He renews *people* (Titus 3:5). Therefore, that creative power is available to us.

With people, the Spirit has two creative functions: First, to make unsaved people new (John 3:3, the new birth). This doesn't mean new in contrast to old but in contrast to what never existed before. Believers are born again into a creatively new life. Indeed, the Bible calls this a "new creation" (2 Cor. 5:17), an action so revolutionary that God calls the individual a "new self" (Eph. 4:24).

The second creative function of the Spirit deals with those who are already believers. Ezekiel's vision of the "temple river," the stream that flowed from the temple in Jerusalem toward the Arabah, is a description of the Spirit's work in us: "Where the river flows everything will live" (Ezek. 47:9). The Spirit renews, revives, and refreshes us. The Bible calls these experiences revivals (Ps. 85:6). Our success in Christian living depends upon the frequency and strength of these renewals. If we have them occasionally or not at all, we will slide backward to the level of the natural life. Defeat means living on the level of the old pre-creation life, and that leads to frustration and discouragement.

We will never retreat as long as the Spirit is free to be creatively alive in us. Can you imagine Him dry or barren? When He is in charge, we walk in His strength, tap His energy, and accomplish more for God and people. If we want to reach our fullest potential, we must let Him renew us, this wonderful Holy Spirit, whose work always has been—and always will be—*renewal!*

The Spirit gives life (John 6:63).

God's Love Song

The Bible teaches self-esteem, but it teaches it realistically. To build self-esteem on our own resources and abilities is to set ourselves up for a fall. Self-esteem is directly related to divine esteem; the greater our understanding of how God feels about us, the greater our self-esteem will be.

How does God feel about us? "The Lord your God is with you, he is mighty to save. He will take great delight in you, he will quiet you with his love, he will rejoice over you with singing" (Zeph. 3:17). This is the only biblical reference to God singing [except for Jesus, when He sang a psalm with His disciples (Mark 14:26)]. All the signs of high esteem are there—God is with us, He delights in us, He soothes us with His love, He sings over us.

This is only one of many expressions of God's esteem of us. We are in His thoughts (Ps. 40:5, KJV). In spite of circumstances, "The Lord thinketh upon me" (v. 17, KJV). The "saints" are the "glorious ones in whom is all my delight" (Ps.

16:3). As a lover holds the image of his beloved in his mind, so God holds us. Jesus startles us with the words, "That the world may know that thou hast sent me, and hast loved them, as thou hast loved me" (John 17:23, KJV). Loved—as much as the Son! Also, God knows us intimately, even watching over us before our birth (Ps. 139:15-16). This shows how high is God's interest in us, His joy in seeing us grow, a delight that we *are*.

God's esteem for us generates a reflexive action—we think more highly of ourselves. We are loved by the supreme Person of the universe. We are prepared-for, planned-for people, not accidents of nature or freaks of biology. We are God-imaged persons, headed for an eternal relationship with God. God's tremendous esteem for us enabled Him to provide us a Savior—Jesus—and a salvation which clothes us again with favor. No wonder Paul bursts out in praise:

Oh, the depth of the riches of the wisdom and knowledge of God! (Rom. 11:33).

Christians Are Born to Win

What are Christians born for? Certainly not to lose! Jesus didn't die on Calvary to found a lost cause. I can't imagine Him giving up or wringing His hands in despair. As far as He is concerned, ultimate victory is assured.

Our job is to tap that confidence and draw it to where we live. To do this we must realize what a Christian is. A Christian believes in Christ, follows Christ. Most importantly, a Christian has Christ residing within. This fact makes all the difference in the

13

world. For example, an infant represents total helplessness and dependence. But every child also represents a human being with a full capacity for growth and maturity. Likewise, a newly born Christian is a baby Christian, but God expects him to develop into a fully grown, fully matured disciple of His Son. The equipment necessary to bring this about is right there. Strong, healthy Christian living doesn't come from the outside—a magic formula, a surprise benefit—but from within. And the Christ who lives within us is not defeatable.

Augustine of Hippo was converted in A.D. 386 after a long struggle with God. He had been plagued by intellectual pride and physical lust. Once converted, however, he grew strong and robust in faith. One of his key verses was Galatians 2:20, "Christ liveth in me" (KJV). One day he met one of his former mistresses who called out to him. Augustine replied, "I am not the same Augustine. I am a new person. Christ now lives in me."

"Christ in us" is adequate for any and every kind of experience we will ever face. How refreshing and heartening! Christ is not in the business of producing losers but winners. Therefore, if we trust Him, He will propel us to victory.

In all these things we are more than conquerors through him who loved us (Rom. 8:37).

A Message for Burnouts

Moses was burned out! He tried to liberate his people from Egyptian slavery but failed miserably. Even his own people rejected him, forcing him to flee for his life. Forty years later God brought him to the slopes of Mount Sinai and showed him a bush which crackled with fire, yet was not consumed. Moses stopped and pondered the "strange sight" (Ex. 3:3). God's message was clear: Moses must return to Egypt and free the Israelites—but he must do it in God's power, not his own. Whenever we try to do God's will in our own power, we will be consumed. When it's done in His power, the necessary fuel is always supplied.

There is a difference between weariness and burnout. Jesus was often weary with His travels and ministries, but never of doing the Father's will. He could say of Himself, "Zeal for your house consumes me" (Ps. 69:9), and at the same time say, "My food is to do the will of him who sent me" (John 4:34). Burnout, however, is acute inadequacy to do God's will. Jesus never reached that point. He poured Himself out for others without stint during His lifetime, then "poured out his life unto death" for us (Isa. 53:12). What a ministry! Yet all was accomplished by the Father's power.

I asked a person whose ministry was yielding much fruit for the Lord, "What is your secret? Hard work? Abundant help?" He replied: "Not really. I surrendered everything to the Lord, and now I feel as if I'm on the sidelines watching Him work!" He reminded me of a burning bush—no matter how busy or hectic things were, the oil still flowed.

The "burning-bush principle" is very simple: do only God's will, trust only God's power. Then when the bush burns, it is not consumed.

We have this treasure in jars of clay to show that this all-surpassing power is from God and not from us. We are hard pressed on every side, but not crushed; perplexed, but not in despair; persecuted, but not abandoned; struck down, but not destroyed (2 Cor. 4:7-9).

The Power
of Trifles

Most of the joys in the Christian life come from little things. These joys are very personal. God deals with us in such uniquely individual ways that He keeps "secrets" with us. They become a language between God and us in which the communication is private. This makes the joy of trifles a rich joy indeed.

Remember when Jesus looked at Peter (Luke 22:61)? That look meant nothing to the other disciples, but everything to Peter! That's why an answer to prayer, while ordinary to others, is a miracle to the one who uttered it. The Lord's messages usually come to us in a faint whispering voice (1 Kings 19:12). We often miss the communication because we listen for the trumpet blast instead of the thin chime from heaven. God's joys are found in the infinitesimal!

However, while God's trifles are tiny, they are never inconsequential. "Who despises the day of small things?" (Zech. 4:10). Goliath took one look at David's youth and his five smooth stones and roared out insults at him. But look what happened to Goliath! Hudson Taylor once wrote: "The financial balance for the entire China Inland Mission yesterday was twenty-five cents. Praise the Lord! Twenty-five cents plus all the promises of God." To Taylor, twenty-five cents was not where God ended His work but where He began it.

Jesus was grateful for trifles like widows' mites, a few fish, a few loaves of bread. What opportunities they gave Him! We should rejoice in limited means and little strength because these are the minute drops that together fill our cups to overflowing. The key is not the amounts, but the God who supplies them. Didn't an ordinary desert bush burst ablaze with God's glory (Ex. 3:1-2)? Can't God make a humdrum marriage, a tedious job, a small ministry glow with His glory so that we catch our breath and weep and worship? That's the joy of trifles—to see God's might in the minuscule!

Here is a boy with five small barley loaves and two small fish, but how far will they go among so many? (John 6:9).

The Food of Faith

Faith, like love, must be nourished to survive. But the food required is totally different. Love thrives on response and acceptance; in short, love thrives on love. But faith thrives on difficulty and testing. Peter calls these things "the trial of your faith" (1 Pet. 1:7, KJV), and makes it clear that such trials strengthen our faith and make it glorious.

While faith can channel enormous power (even removing mountains), by itself it is quite fragile. Like a column of mercury, it rises or falls in moment-by-moment sensitivity to its surroundings. Sometimes we find ourselves possessing a faith that can conquer all; at other times it is so puny the smallest problems terrify us. That's why faith can't be taken for granted. It needs attention, care and, above all, nourishment.

Where does faith's nourishment come from? The *Word.* "Faith comes by hearing, and hearing by the word of God" (Rom. 10:17, NKJV). The Word contains the food our faith most often needs—assurance. By feeding on the promises, faith gains strength and matures.

Faith's nourishment also comes from *trials.* George Muller called adversity "the food of faith." He pointed out that believers often try to avoid trials by resorting to natural ways of solving their difficulties, thus cutting off the means by which faith is strengthened. Instead, said Muller, if we trusted God to help us in our difficulties (which are always "for a little while," 1 Pet. 1:6), we would not only emerge triumphantly but would be better positioned to face the next round of testing.

In adversity, faith has two options: to escape it the best way possible; or accept it as a challenge from God to enable us to triumph. Let us try to win the commendation of Jesus, "Great is your faith!" (Matt. 15:28, NKJV). Then we will experience double joy—the joy of having a strong faith and the joy of our Lord's approval.

Fear of man will prove to be a snare, but whoever trusts in the Lord is kept safe (Prov. 29:25).

All in God's Time

Jesus Christ always obeyed the Father's will, and always in the Father's way. Also, He did it always in the Father's time. J. G. Bellet said, "Christ was always mindful of God's rights." One of those rights was time. The transfiguration of Jesus (Luke 9) not only shows us His Deity, it shows us how He regarded the Father's schedule. The decision given Him on the mount was not that He must die (that had already been settled), but when—"Go now!" So He resolutely "set his face to go to Jerusalem" (v. 51, RSV).

The Father's timing was important to Jesus because God always acts when the time is ripe. "When the time had fully come, God sent his Son" (Gal. 4:4). There is only one time to do anything—God's—which is always set for the perfect moment. To reject His timing is to reject His wisdom.

Our sensitivity to God's time, however, should not make us clock-watchers or time-servers. It is not time itself that we should be concerned with, but God's *use* of it. This means we must be careful students of time's Creator. Unless we move in rhythm with the Father, feeling and seeing things as He does, all of His actions will seem out of joint. When we say, "Why didn't He answer sooner?" we are admitting that we are out of step with Him. When we grow impatient because the answer has not yet come, we are challenging either His concern or wisdom, or both. The key to the mastery of time is to know and understand God. The acceptance of His timing comes naturally to the man or woman deeply devoted to Him.

How often we are fussy about our schedules! A missed plane, an unscheduled overnight stay fill us with irritation. We are not "mindful of God's rights." Jesus cleared the decks of His life for one purpose—to give God His rights. When we accept God's schedule, we acknowledge His authority over us. Then we learn that there is "a time for every matter under heaven" (Eccl. 3:1, RSV).

In the beginning, O Lord, you laid the foundations of the earth. . . . But you remain the same, and your years will never end (Heb. 1:10,12).

The Mind
of Christ

To walk in fellowship with Jesus, we must walk in agreement with Him. "Can two walk together, unless they are agreed?" (Amos 3:3, NKJV). A person cannot be saved unless he or she agrees with Christ. Speaking personally, I accepted His truths, believed His teachings, and agreed with what He said about Himself (He was the Savior) and about me (I was a sinner). Salvation is impossible without this initial agreement and acceptance.

In our walk as Christians, we must still agree with Him. The Christian life is a daily adjusting to His mind, a daily agreeing with what He teaches us, a daily accepting of His will. The moment we disagree, that moment our fellowship ruptures. Continued disagreement only widens the breach until we come back to the point of agreeing with Him once again—which is what confession is (see 1 John 1:9).

Agreement is one of life's basic facts. The pilot must agree with the air traffic controllers; the captain who pilots a ship must agree with the charts of his course. All life is adjustment, and the Christian life is no different. If we want fellowship with Jesus, we must bend continually to His mind and heart. We must think what He thinks, look where He is looking, and move in the direction He is moving. Like Philip, we must be ready at a moment's notice to leave our work in Samaria to find someone on the southern road who needs Jesus. God's eternal plan never changes, but the daily adjustments to that plan do. We must continually live in agreement with Him.

Living in agreement with Christ leads to a life of rich joy. Its utter simplicity affords joy! W. L. Pettingill once said: "The Christian life is the easiest of all—only one Person to please, only one thing to do." It frees us from the tension of having to prove ourselves. We are His, joyfully His, and inward rest follows the realization of this fact.

Take my yoke upon you and learn from me . . . and you will find rest (Matt. 11:29).

Tall Enough to Stoop

Is God limited? No. He is never limited in the things He wants to do. David said: "You stoop down to make me great" (Ps. 18:35). The idea here is one of condescension: You lower Yourself to make me great. It's the precursor of God's incarnation in Christ who made Himself "nothing," who "humbled himself and became obedient to death—even death on a cross!" (Phil. 2:7-8). Think of it, God stooping, humbling Himself, all for our benefit!

God's stooping is necessary. If He hadn't stooped, we could never have been saved. Jesus stooped to become man, then He stooped further to become a sinbearer to make salvation possible. God's stooping also makes fellowship with Him possible. "For this is what the high and lofty One says—he who lives forever, whose name is holy: 'I live in a high and holy place, but also with him who is contrite and lowly in spirit'" (Isa. 57:15). God lowers Himself because we could never approach Him on our own merits. "He knows how we are formed, he remembers that we are dust" (Ps. 103:14).

What a message for us! We too must be ready to stoop if we want to be worthy disciples of Him who stooped for us. Stooping means: "I see your need and have come alongside to help." It also means: "I will not ignore nor run away from the hurts of people around me." Let's avoid detours that prevent us from ministering to others, whether they are prejudices, pride, or whatever. The essential thing is—we must stoop! This is the beginning of God's ministry to us; it is also the beginning of our ministry to each other. May God make us tall enough to stoop, strong enough to submit, and lofty enough to be humble. Then, like God, we'll "heal the brokenhearted and bind up their wounds" (Ps. 147:3).

Humble yourselves before the Lord, and he will lift you up (Jas. 4:10).

"No-Offense" Disciples

Whenever we are angry, bitter, or worried, our relationship to Jesus suffers. One Indonesian missionary grew angry because the natives were stealing his pineapples. God showed him that he was not demonstrating Christ to the natives; he was in the awkward predicament of denying, by anger, the very gospel he was trying to preach. He needed to become a "no-offense" disciple, one who refused to be upset by the treatment of the world. Is this possible? The psalmist thought so. He said, "Great peace have they who love your law, and nothing can make them stumble [upset them]" (Ps. 119:165).

Speaking honestly, being offended is a state of mind that refuses to accept circumstances that belittle, embarrass, or cause pain. Jesus said we cannot escape offensive situations, but we can learn to react positively to them (Matt. 18:7). The solution is to become a "no-offense" disciple. If everything does indeed work together for good (Rom. 8:28), then we have no excuse for being offended. And if we do become offended, our offendedness really amounts to a rejection of God's lordship over our lives. In other words, Romans 8:28 takes away our right to be offended at any kind of treatment we might receive. We can't call Jesus Lord, then fume at the way He leads us!

When Obadiah Holmes, an early New England Baptist, was tied to the stocks and beaten for holding an unauthorized prayer meeting in the Boston area, he turned afterward to his punishers and said, "You have struck me as with roses!" Holmes was a "no-offense" disciple! If we have a "no-offense" heart, all God's discipline will be by "roses."

The only time the Bible allows us to take offense is when Jesus is dishonored. In this case, we are offended for His sake, we bear His "reproach" (Heb. 13:13, KJV). To take offense for His sake is an honor; to take it for our own sake is not.

I am the Lord your God, who teaches you what is best for you, who directs you in the way you should go (Isa. 48:17).

The Source of Our Strength

The old Hebrew warrior, Caleb, was one of the spies who brought back a good report from the land of Canaan (Num. 13). As a reward, he was promised an inheritance in the new land. Forty-five years later, after Israel invaded Canaan, Caleb asked for his inheritance. He said to Joshua: "I'm just as vigorous to go out to battle now as I was then. . . . the Lord helping me, I will drive them out" (Josh. 14:11-12). Caleb's confidence was based upon strength, but not his own. Behind his natural strength was God's. So Caleb went forth, conquered, and won his inheritance.

The lesson Caleb teaches us is: We may have natural ability, but just the same we must rely on God. How inviting it is to fall back on easy self-reliance! We've had experience, so we say, "That's not so difficult, I've done it before." Or we have training, so we say, "I'm ready for that particular job." Or we have talent, so we say, "I've got it in me."

But *every* experience for God is *new*, and every job must be tackled as if for the first time. I remember an older preacher's prayer: "O Lord, help me to lean on You now as I did when I first began, when I depended upon You for every thought!" Wisely, he remembered the Source of his enabling strength.

To rely on God's strength means we must deny our natural tendency to fall back on our own strength. Spiritual people may use their strength, but they go far beyond it and rely on the One who said, "Is anything too hard for the Lord?" (Gen. 18:14). In a sense, as Paul did, the spiritual person treats his own strength as weakness in order that through God his weakness might become strength. The natural man always tries to squeeze by by being clever enough. The spiritual person humbly trusts the Mighty One and "rides the high places of the earth."

Now to him who is able to do immeasurably more than all we ask or imagine, according to his power that is at work within us (Eph. 3:20).

Becoming Sensitive to Others

We often pray, "Lord, make us sensitive to the needs of others." And often God has allowed this prayer to go flat. We must realize that we can't *pray* ourselves into sensitivity for others. Instead, we must move into a closer relationship with Him. Who is more sensitive to human need than God? (Heb. 4:14-16; 1 Pet. 5:7). The closer we walk with Him, the more sensitive we will grow toward others.

If our sensitivity stems merely from people's needs, we will become either fanatics or hopeless drudges. The Lord's sensitivity doesn't grow out of human need, it grows out of His character. "As a father has compassion on his children, so the Lord has compassion on those who fear him; for he knows how we are formed, he remembers that we are dust" (Ps. 103:13-14). A father's sympathy is not as much aroused by scraped knees as it is by his *son's* scraped knees, a sympathy that grows out of his fatherhood. This kind of sensitivity is built into the relationship. So it is with our Heavenly Father and us.

Isaiah did not need to pray, "Lord, make me sensitive." He needed only to gaze at the high and lofty One, then cry out, "Here am I, send me" (Isa. 6:8). As wax melts in the sun's presence, Isaiah's heart melted in deep pity for his people simply by being in the Lord's presence. I have seen hardened people become so sensitized by their new relationship to Jesus that the mere thought of the world's lostness moved them to tears. These are the tears of God for a lost world.

If we keep on asking God to make us sensitive, we are really saying that we're really not close to God. We live at a distance from Him. How sensitive Jesus was and how indescribably close to the Father did He live! Closeness to God and sensitivity to people go hand in hand.

Everyone who loves [others] has been born of God and knows God. Whoever does not love does not know God, because God is love (1 John 4:7-8).

Present-Tense Deliverance

Sometimes we have too narrow a view of deliverance. We often look upon it as extrication from circumstances. But in God's eyes, deliverance is in the circumstance itself. When Joseph tried to escape from the temptress, Potiphar's wife, he landed in prison

(Gen. 39). Where was God's deliverance? God had promised to make him a prince, but he became a prisoner! Not only was there no deliverance, his circumstances were getting worse!

However, Joseph's string of degrading experiences ended while in prison. He interpreted Pharaoh's dream and, in gratitude, the king elevated him to a position of power and honor next to his own throne (Gen. 41:40). The prince had finally arrived! Joseph's entire life shows how God's deliverance of His children is intertwined with the painful circumstances in which they find themselves.

The difference between the trials of the natural person and the trials of the spiritual person is *redemption*. There is no redemption at work in the trials of the natural person; he is simply suffering the casualty of being human. But the trials of the spiritual person have God actively and presently at work in them to make those trials the *seed* out of which deliverance comes. God never delivers us *from* trials (though it may seem so); He delivers us *with* trials. The trial itself is the necessary instrument which He uses to bring about the deliverance. This means that deliverance is present, continuous, ongoing, and relevant. It is never idle nor ceasing. Therefore, Annie Johnson Flint was correct when she wrote:

> He's helping me now—this moment,
>   Though I may not see it or hear,
> Perhaps by a friend far distant,
>   Perhaps by a stranger near,
> Perhaps by a spoken message,
>   Perhaps by the printed word;
> In ways that I know—and know not,
>   I have the help of the Lord.

God is our refuge and strength, an ever-present help in trouble (Ps. 46:1).

Wholeness

God is in the business of developing whole people. Paul says, "May God himself... sanctify you through and through. May your whole spirit, soul and body be kept blameless at the coming of our Lord Jesus Christ" (1 Thess. 5:23). Wholeness isn't sinlessness but consistency between our inner and outer life. Psychologists call this "integrity." The Bible uses words like *perfect* and *whole*. Jesus doesn't redeem part of us; He makes us entirely whole.

The opposite of wholeness is either *iniquity* or *hypocrisy*. By iniquity I mean that our motives and actions are unclean. By hypocrisy I mean our motives are unclean, but we try to convince others they are not. Of the seven things God "hates" (Prov. 6:16-19), five are actions and two are attitudes. Simply to *do* right is not enough for God, we must have right motives as well. That's wholeness! His aim in redemption is not merely to purge our record of sin but our actions of sin. To do this He must purge our motives, feelings, and thoughts. But there's good news! Christ is able to change what we *are* as well as what we do. "Those who live according to the flesh set their minds on the things of the flesh, but those who live according to the Spirit set their minds on the things of the Spirit" (Rom. 8:5, RSV). You'll note that "being" precedes "doing." An unsaved person, because of his old nature, cannot do things that please God. On the other hand, a Spirit-filled person can easily do the things that please God because the new nature has taken hold. In order to be whole (thinking and doing things which please God), we must "live by the Spirit [under the Spirit's control], and you will not gratify the desires of the sinful nature" (Gal. 5:16).

God's ability to make us whole cuts away the usual criticism of Christianity—that it's a beautiful but unworkable ideal. God not only wants wholeness, He "qualifies" us to become whole via His power. What a God, and what a redemption!

**Put off your old self... [and] put on the new self, created to
be like God in true righteousness and holiness
(Eph. 4:22-23).**

Commitment

"Father, into your hands I commit my spirit" (Luke 23:46).
This touching submission marked Jesus' final moments on Calvary before He died. It was, of course, a submission unto *death*.
And yet, when I ponder the psalm from which Jesus quoted
these words, I am struck by the fact that Jesus was uttering the
guiding principle of His life.

The original statement comes from David, "Into your hands I
commit my spirit" (Ps. 31:5). This was David's commitment to
God of his *life*. He was not at the point of death but rather in the
full, bustling excitement of life. True, he was surrounded by
enemies, but instead of expecting the end, he looked for victory
through God's power. The closing refrain says, "Be strong and
take heart, all you who hope in the Lord" (v. 24). The whole
psalm is one of dedication: "Lord, I give myself to You, spirit,
times, and life; therefore I hope in You for victory" (vv. 4-5,15-
16). David's commitment was total—for life and for death.

Jesus followed the same pattern. He said to His critics: "I
always do what pleases him [the Father]" (John 8:29). He lived
to please His Father in time, life, and spirit. When dying, it was
only natural that He should commit His spirit to Him then as He
had done in life. George Whitefield, the eighteenth-century evangelist, echoed this when he said: "I give up myself to be a martyr
for Him who hung on the Cross for me. I have thrown myself
blindfolded and, I trust, without reserve into His almighty
hands."

John Wycliffe said, "Christ's deeds and examples are commandments of what we should do." As Jesus yielded His life, so should we. This means a full surrender of our spirit, time, strength, loved ones—in short, our all. Though we stumble, our aim must be the same as that of Jesus. Don't fear! God will "equip [us] with everything good for doing his will" (Heb. 13:21)!

Therefore, I urge you, brothers, in view of God's mercy, to offer your bodies as living sacrifices, holy and pleasing to God (Rom. 12:1).

Tapping the Fullness of God

Can we ever comprehend the fullness of God? Of course not. But amazingly, we can tap what we can't understand and use daily what is a perfect mystery to us. Here's what I mean:

Charles H. Spurgeon, the noted London preacher, was on his way home after a tiring day. He was weary and depressed. Like a flash, the text came to him: "My grace is sufficient for thee." When he arrived home, he looked up the Greek text and it read, "MY grace is sufficient for thee." He said, "I should think it is, Lord" and burst out laughing. Unbelief seemed so absurd, like a little fish worrying lest the Thames River would not be enough for him, or a mouse in Egypt, after the seven years of plenty, fearing he would die of famine. Or a man living on a mountain afraid he would run out of oxygen.

Yes, absurd, isn't it? That's why it is important for us to grasp the meaning of the fullness of God. Like many other Christians, I have always believed in God's sufficiency, but there's a great difference between mentally acknowledging it and tapping into it for my daily needs.

Jesus showed us how to live. He was conscious of the Father's fullness at all times. Even more, He knew that the Father would use that fullness to meet His needs, such as for miracles, teaching great truths, and even His atoning work on Calvary.

God invites us to tap His endless resources for our needs also. "God is able to make all grace abound to you, so that in all things at all times . . . you will abound in every good work" (2 Cor. 9:8). The "abounding" occurs when we do three things:

1. Accept God's resources as adequate for our needs;

2. Rely on those resources whenever we need them;

3. Joyfully expect God to act, and stop worrying whether He will or not.

[We] are abundantly satisfied with the fullness of Your house,
And You give [us] drink from the river of Your pleasures
(Ps. 36:8, NKJV).

Simplicity

If we know Jesus, we will be drawn to living the simple life. Does this mean a life without posessions? Not necessarily. It is a life in which possessions have no rank. Teresa of Avila, the sixteenth-century Spanish mystic, said: "Let our houses be small and poor in every way. Let us to some extent resemble our King, Who had no house save the porch in Bethlehem where He was born and the cross on which He died." Does this mean espousing the vow of poverty? Not really. It means we must use things "as if [they] were not [ours] to keep" (1 Cor. 7:30). The simple life boils down to a simple rule: God is my chief desire—"Seek first his kingdom and his righteousness" (Matt. 6:33). Our focus must be God Himself, how to please and serve Him. Material things should never become our focus because anxiety about them is the worst anxiety of all.

The simple life is single-visioned. Jesus said, "If . . . thine eye be single [*aplous*, fixed on one object], thy whole body shall be full of light" (Matt. 6:22, KJV). Physically, our eyes cannot focus on two things at once; neither can our spiritual eyes. Is this difficult? Not at all. Single-minded believers are free from tension and distraction. They are like arrows bent on a target. They will not meander or dawdle. They will refuse to make permanent what God calls transitory, and transitory what God calls eternal. For this reason, the simple life is the easy life. François Fénelon said: "O how amiable this simplicity is! Who will give it to me? I will leave all for this. It is the pearl of the Gospel."

The opposite of the simple life—the selfish life—is the most exhausting, frustrating, and disillusioning of all. Let's not be guilty of short vision and wrong priorities. God values us too highly to lose us in that way!

The blessing of the Lord makes one rich, And He adds no sorrow with it (Prov. 10:22, NKJV).

God Knows Us Perfectly

David's statement, "O Lord, you have searched me and you know me" (Ps. 139:1), reveals God's perfect knowledge of us. In our lifetime we ask hundreds of questions, but God never needs to ask one. His perfect knowledge of us should make us humble. There is no place for hypocrisy in our relationship with Him. God can't be deceived.

How encouraging to read that God searches us and knows us. He is omniscient, which means His knowledge of us is personal. He understands our thoughts. He is acquainted with all our ways. Such a knowledge of us by a fellow human being would be devastating, but God's all-knowing is balanced by His love: "God *so* loved." His love prevents Him from turning His omniscience into a weapon of cruelty or a chain of slavery. We need not fear that God knows the *worst* about us. He already knew this long before we were born, yet still He sent His Son to save us from our "worsts."

God knows us, but, best of all, He loves us! Therefore we must not be afraid to pray: "Search me, O God, and know my heart: try me, and know my thoughts: And see if there be any wicked way in me" (vv. 23-24, KJV). God's searching leads His children to cleansing, not judgment. We must allow Him to search us because this is the basis of continued fellowship with Him. Of course He finds imperfection in us, but how can we improve unless He shows us our flaws?

What God seeks from us is an earnest desire to please Him. Perfection is beyond our reach, but desire, holy desire, is possible for us all. This desire is implanted by the Holy Spirit. Therefore, God looks for the fruit of the Spirit to appear in us.

I obey your statutes, for I love them greatly. I obey your precepts and your statutes, for all my ways are known to you (Ps. 119:167-68).

The Human Side of Being a Christian

Christianity has suffered from two criticisms: One, it stresses a perfection which no human can attain. Second, it denies our innate humanity. Wrong on both counts! God does prod us toward holiness, but He also provides for failure. "If anyone sins, we have an Advocate with the Father" (1 John 2:1, NKJV). Does it deny our humanity? The truth is that the Christian is more fully human than his unsaved counterpart.

The gospel doesn't destroy the appetites of the body; it puts them to proper use. True, food may lead to gluttony, but food is necessary. Sex may lead to fornication, but sex is necessary for the future of the race. We are not to crucify these appetites, but *regulate* them. The flesh, on the other hand, must be "crucified" (Gal. 5:24). That's because the flesh can't be regulated or controlled (Rom. 8:6-8). Such attitudes as pride, lust, covetousness, jealousy, hatred, bitterness, contentiousness, and so forth are totally harmful. They are deadly and are obstacles to both our human and spiritual fulfillment.

Let's be careful, however, not to blame the flesh for what is natural to human beings. It is human to be ambitious, and this is acceptable if it is not tainted by the flesh. To be ambitious to serve God is a wholesome ambition, but to be ambitious to be the head of the company, by fair means or foul, is of the flesh. Self-esteem is admirable if it means giving glory to God for what He has enabled us to be. But to glorify ourselves is the flesh all over. To boast is not wrong if we boast in the right thing (as Paul did about the cross, Gal. 6:14). To boast *of* ourselves and *in* ourselves is an odious outcropping of the flesh.

So we must distinguish three things: the lusts of the flesh, the desires of the body, and the qualities of being human. The flesh must be crucified, the body must be regulated, and the human side of us must be encouraged. May the Lord give us the mind of Christ about all three!

Live by the Spirit, and you will not gratify the desires of the sinful nature (Gal. 5:16).

Renewing Our Spiritual Energy

Like physical energy, spiritual energy must be renewed. Ministry is depleting and, to a certain extent, so is fellowship with others. The key to renewing our spiritual vitality is to keep in touch with Jesus. The Lord underscored this when He said to His disciples, "Remain in me" (John 15:4). To abide in Christ means more than a fleeting glance in His direction or an occasional look into His word. Jesus meant: stay in close, living communion with Me; keep drawing from Me all you need, and don't rely on yourself or anyone else to keep spiritually renewed. To neglect Jesus and lose our communion with Him means to become dry brush fit only to be cut, gathered, and thrown into the fire (v. 6).

How easy ministry for Jesus becomes when we do what He asks of us. Do we need more love? There is all the love we'll ever need in Jesus. Do we long to be more patient and tolerant with those who are irksome? He has abounding patience we can tap. Do we want to be more fruitful in winning others to Him, in seeing disciples grow stronger in their faith and love? Fruit will grow in abundance as long as we are attached to the Vine. If we keep drawing, He will keep giving until needs are met and our spirits are satisfied. Just as Jesus, the ever-vibrant Vine, teemed with life and power to share with others, so will we if we remain connected to Him as the branch does to the vine.

To abound we must abide! One of the unique laws of nature is that as the branch lives to feed others, it feeds itself. Spiritually, as we become channels of Christ's life to others, we ourselves benefit from that life. We become spiritually renewed not merely by taking Christ in, but by giving Him out to others. This constant sharing does not result in depletion, but a continual renewal, as Paul described it, "As dying, and, behold, we live" (2 Cor. 6:9, KJV).

If a man remains in me and I in him, he will bear much fruit; apart from me you can do nothing (John 15:5).

Living Above Fatigue

We need to learn that the Holy Spirit has a unique relationship to our bodies. When we believe in Christ, the Holy Spirit comes to live inside us. When we become physically worn and tired, the Spirit can revive us with new vigor. "If the Spirit of him who raised Jesus from the dead is living in you, he who raised Christ from the dead will also give life to your mortal bodies through his Spirit who lives in you" (Rom. 8:11). This means our bodies as well as our spirits are under the laws of the Spirit.

A dead battery cannot start a car motor, but if we connect a new battery to the old, the old will become recharged and send out power as before. This is what the Lord says about our bodies: "They that wait upon the Lord shall renew their strength; they shall mount up with wings as eagles; they shall run, and not be weary; and they shall walk, and not faint" (Isa. 40:31, KJV).

Waiting on the Lord releases the Spirit's power in us, and He infuses our bodies with new energy. Best of all, we don't get weary doing it!

A. B. Simpson was a pastor in Kentucky who suffered acutely from heart, lung, asthmatic, and nervous troubles. He was constantly ill, and a few times was close to death. While on vacation in Old Orchard, Maine, Simpson heard a Bible teacher explain the relationship between the Spirit and our bodies and His ability to quicken them. Later Simpson sought the privacy of a nearby woods and there turned his body over to God, asking for the quickening of his strength. God responded and filled him with new life. Simpson lived to a ripe old age, was never again bothered by physical limitations, and became one of the busiest, most productive servants of God in the nineteenth century.

You are not your own; you were bought at a price. Therefore honor God with your body (1 Cor. 6:19-20).

Turning Rubbish into Glory

Nehemiah teaches us where God begins His work—with rubbish. He also teaches us where God ends it—with glory. Nehemiah journeyed from Persia to Jerusalem to rebuild its broken walls (Neh. 1). When he arrived he found the people in fear and the walls in rubble (2:17). He had no glorious vision with which to begin; he only had rubbish. But isn't this how God always begins? Out of the "formless and empty" earth He made a beautiful planet (Gen. 1:2). Out of the rubbish of idolatry, Israel was formed into a nation of beauty (Ezek. 16:1-8). Out of the rubbish of pagan practices, the church became an assembly of saints (1 Cor. 6:9-11).

The gospel transforms rubbish-pile people into specimens of God's glory. As in Nehemiah's day, Satan loves to point to the dusty pile of ruins and say, "You mean you're going to do something with *that?*" But we answer him with Nehemiah's words: "The God of heaven will give us success" (Neh. 2:20). This is the beginning of the end of rubbish!

Sanctification is the process of changing the rubbish of self into the glory of godliness. When George Muller was asked about his success as a Christian, he replied: "There was a day when I died to George Muller, his opinions, preferences, tastes and will." That is, the rubbish had to go before Muller could display God's holiness. Paul's rubbish was the religious kind: "a Hebrew of Hebrews . . . a Pharisee; as for zeal, persecuting the church; as for legalistic righteousness, faultless" (Phil. 3:5-6). But he declared it all "rubbish, that I may gain Christ" (v. 8).

God can build no glorious work in us until we allow Him to scrape away all the rubbish that chokes our hearts. We must let Him dig us clean, polish us, and remake us until we are "precious stones" (Isa. 54:12) to Him. It is His beauty, not ours; it is His power, not our weakness.

The splendor I had given you made your beauty perfect (Ezek. 16:14).

Loving Ourselves

There is a difference between loving ourselves self-centeredly and loving ourselves properly. Self-centered love kept the rich young man from following Jesus (Mark 10:17-22). He loved his possessions more than Christ because his possessions were simply an extension of himself. This kind of self-love is destructive; it seeks to please only the self. On the other hand, the proper kind of self-love seeks to please God.

True self-love begins at Calvary. Paul says, "I live by faith in the Son of God, who loved *me* and gave himself for *me*" (Gal. 2:20, emphasis added). The love that Jesus showed for us at Calvary was not group love but personal love. He loves us all as individuals, not as a race. He loves us as the unique, different, one-of-a-kind person each of us is. This means He loves my soul, my self, my ego. I must not deny this highly personal love, but accept it and thank Him for it. I must go farther: I must agree with this kind of love, and love the very self which He loves. Because I love myself and want the best for myself, I yield to Jesus as my Savior, thus ensuring an immortality with Him. My conversion, therefore, is a form of self-love, but it is the proper kind of self-love—it loves what God loves.

In addition, I must love myself to such an extent that I yield myself fully to the Lordship of Jesus Christ in order to attain the potential that He has in mind for me. If I am His "workmanship" (Eph. 2:10), then I am wise if I accept His control of my life and allow Him to bring me up to my fullest flowering in Him. This is self-love properly expressed. It is not self-love squandered foolishly upon myself, but rather filled to the fullest by an alliance with Jesus, who loves me that I might love myself properly.

This is my responsibility: to love God first and seek His glory; to love others next and seek their best good; and to love myself last and seek God's eternal friendship.

What good is it for a man to gain the whole world, yet forfeit his soul? Or what can a man give in exchange for his soul? (Mark 8:36-37).

Responding to Pressure

I recently talked to a pastor from Rajahmundry, India, who said that the sandalwood tree of his native land is full of perfume. The more it is cut, the more perfume it yields. The well-known Indian Christian Sadhu Sundar Singh said: "Every Christian should be like the sandalwood tree, imparting fragrance to the axe which cuts it."

Reactions reveal! A friend writes, "One of the women in our church gave a talk about a lemon. She described it as having a beautiful color, interesting texture, and so forth, very pleasant to look at. But when the lemon is cut and pressure is applied, the juice it produces is very sour." So we may look appealing on the outside, but when pressure is applied we may respond with a sour attitude. My friend continued, "It isn't the pressure which makes the lemon sour; the sourness was there all along. The pressure just brought it out."

Bad attitudes are not learned from without, they are developed from within. Jesus said, "From within, out of men's hearts, come evil thoughts" (Mark 7:21). Bad attitudes can also be made worse by bad experiences, but the raw material is already there.

To react sweetly to all kinds of circumstances means we must be inwardly sweet. The gospel is useless unless it transforms us inside. Rejoice that Jesus is not a "Pharisee" Savior. He came to clean the inside of the cup as well as the outside. There is nothing so exhausting as pretense. We need the relaxation of wholeness, the serenity of a life in which the "mind of Christ" (1 Cor. 2:16) purifies our inner thoughts as well as our outward reactions. Then we'll become one of the Lord's sandalwood trees!

---

*Whatever is true, whatever is noble, whatever is right, what-
ever is pure, whatever is lovely, whatever is admirable—
if anything is excellent or praiseworthy—think about
such things. . . . And the God of peace will be with you
(Phil. 4:8-9).*

The Seeming "Snubs" of Jesus

A Canaanite woman came to Jesus to ask Him to heal her demon-possessed daughter (Matt. 15:21-28), but Jesus snubbed her. Undaunted, she pursued His disciples so relentlessly that they urged Him, "Send her away, for she keeps crying out after us." But Jesus replied, "I was sent only to the lost sheep of Israel." Surely this would have put her off! But no, she kept after Him. She fell at His feet and said, "Lord, help me!" Again Jesus held her away: "It is not right to take the children's bread and toss it to their dogs." Surely this would discourage her! But she replied, "Yes, Lord, but even the dogs eat the crumbs that fall from their masters' table." This was enough for Jesus. He said, "Woman, you have great faith! Your request is granted." And her daughter was healed "that very hour."

The Lord blessed this woman beyond her dreams. Instant healing of her child was granted because her faith triumphed over her sensitivity. Jesus deliberately snubbed her to test that faith. If it had been weak, Jesus' snubs would have awakened her touchy feelings, and she would have left angry.

Very often we are like this Canaanite woman, coming to God with a pressing need. But unlike this woman, we sometimes grow discouraged and weary when He does not answer quickly. Our faith retreats. We quail before His "snubs." We say, "It must not be His will." So we rob ourselves of timely blessings because we take the snub as refusal instead of a test of faith and patience.

We need spiritual imagination and pluck; imagination, as William Cowper wrote, to see that "Behind a frowning providence He hides a smiling face." And pluck to stay firm in spite of His seeming aloofness. He longs to bless us if we only persist in faith.

Why are you downcast, O my soul? Why so disturbed within me? Put your hope in God, for I will yet praise him, my Savior and my God (Ps. 42:5-6).

The Personal Side of Our Salvation

Paul was keenly aware of his personal inheritance in Christ. He said, "I press on to take hold of that for which Christ Jesus took hold of me" (Phil. 3:12). He meant, "I want to get everything that's coming to me through Christ." Many of us give up trying to grow spiritually. We get discouraged too easily because of our doubts. We quit too soon.

God's grace produces in us a startling piece of personal salvation. He is not only glorified in the salvation of the church, but also in the individuals who make it up. He does not deal with us à la cookie cutter; we are saved as personally as clay is molded by the potter (Jer. 18:5-6).

There is only one way of salvation—through Christ—and only one condition of receiving it—by faith. But there are as many individual expressions of it as there are believers. That's why

Paul could say, "We are [His] workmanship [*poema*, master-piece], created in Christ Jesus to do good works, which God prepared in advance for us to do" (Eph. 2:10). We are individually called to be personal manifestations of God's power.

This means our spiritual dreams can be fulfilled. Joseph dreamed of being a prince among his brothers. This was not a youthful fantasy but a divine longing planted in his heart at birth. Joel reminds us that the Spirit of God is a creator of visions and dreams (Joel 2:28). Those who are filled with Him are given insight to discern what they can become under His hand and by His power. If we press on with our God-given visions, He will fulfill them in us. We can become what He intends us to be! Arthur Hewitt says, "The man who will trust himself to God is inescapably destined to be blessed above all his own dreams." What greater sense of personal fulfillment can there be than this?

By the grace of God I am what I am, and his grace to me was not without effect (1 Cor. 15:10).

Dealing with Anxiety

Can God help us with our anxiety? The Bible records that even Jesus Himself was anxious: "Now my heart is troubled" (John 12:27). Jesus' anxiety was rooted in His ability to see things as they really were. He knew the nails had sharp points and the cross was real wood. In Gethsemane His anguish was so great He asked the Father to deliver Him from death (Luke 22:42).

But notice how Jesus handled His anxiety. Since the cross was

God's will for Him, He was determined to go through with it. He blunted its pain by the strength of His determination.

This instructs us. When anxious, we must ask a basic question: "Are we in the will of God?" To make God our first concern is to deal properly with whatever anguish threatens us. Our rule must be, as it was for Jesus, "any pain, at any cost, for His sake." Is our pain self-inflicted? Self-inflicted pain occurs when we thrust aside God's will and push forward on our own. Confession is the only way to deal with that pain. However, when the pain is the result of doing God's will, our recourse must be to submit, as Jesus did, and say, "Not my will, but yours be done" (Luke 22:42). As George MacDonald says, "It [self-will] is to be no longer the regent of our action."

Once we submit to God's will, support will be there! When Jesus made the determination to suffer the cross, the Father immediately assured Him by saying, "I have glorified it [my name], and will glorify it again" (John 12:28). Likewise when we realize that doing His will results in greater glory to Him, strength will quickly follow. Support? We'll get all we need from heaven when we turn the key of faith in the lock.

Jesus did not *deny* His anxiety, He accepted it. In doing so He put its outcome squarely into God's hands, who then turned His anxiety into joy.

***Jesus immediately said to them: "Take courage! It is I.
Don't be afraid" (Matt. 14:27).***

Teachableness

When David prayed "teach me your way, O Lord," (Ps. 86:11), he expressed a principle of godly living that is the opposite of the experience of the unsaved person. The natural man doesn't need to be taught how to live the natural life; he lives it by instinct. None of us needs training in how to be selfish. On the other hand, the spiritual person must be carefully instructed how to live the spiritual life. This instruction comes only from God. To become spiritual we must be teachable.

Teachableness, in the words of Jesus, is becoming like "children" (Matt. 11:25). Spiritual children understand God's truth far better than the "wise and learned" of this world. Unless the wise receive a new nature, they will continue to follow the instincts of the natural man, which is no wisdom at all.

Teachableness also means to be free from the obstacles to learning, such as doubt and criticism. If we desire to be taught of the Lord, we must not short-circuit that instruction with rebuttals: "But Lord, what about...?" or "Lord, I don't see how that can be." That's why Jesus said the kingdom of heaven is open only to children (Matt. 18:2-3). Childlikeness is a must to enter the kingdom and grow in it. The natural trustability of children abets their learning and growth. So we must be with our Father if we want to learn His truth.

Since God trains by experience, teachableness also means we must submit to guidance. God led the Israelites through the wilderness "where there is no way" (Ps. 107:40, KJV). So He leads us in strange paths in order to show us how He makes a "way" for us. Above all, we must have faith, for faith is the "beggar attitude," an attitude in which God delights because it enables Him to train us most effectively. Solomon prayed, "I am only a little child. . . . So give your servant a discerning heart." What a prayer for anyone—but especially for the one who longs to be taught by God!

Praise be to you, O Lord; teach me your decrees (Ps. 119:12).

Entering
God's Rest

The Israelites, because of their stubborn ways in the wilderness, did not enter "God's rest." (See Ps. 95:11.) What is God's rest? It is the rest He seeks and the rest He gives. In the Old Testament, the Lord's rest was the temple in Jerusalem. "Arise, O Lord, and come to your resting place" (Ps. 132:8). His rest was being in the central focus of His people. In the New Testament, God's rest is in believers, who are the new temple of God (Eph. 2:22). Basically, God's rest is wherever He is properly honored in the midst of His people.

The rest which God *gives* varies with each of His children, but the principle remains the same. His rest for us is the place where we reach the fulfillment of His will. Abraham sought God's rest in the "city with foundations" (Heb. 11:10), heaven. In this sense heaven is God's absolute rest for all His children. The unsaved find rest in Jesus when they bring their burden of sin and lay it on Him. The rest of the saved is a step beyond—the total commitment to God which results in peace and joy (Heb. 4:9). This rest is like God's sabbath, His rest from labor and effort in creation. The writer urges all believers to seek that rest (v. 11).

Israel failed to reach their rest because they rejected God's ways "in their heart" (Ps. 95:10, KJV). They lost it not because of what they did but because of what they *were*. Likewise, our refusal to do God's will and insistence on our own way causes us to miss the rest He offers. Oswald Chambers says, "Wherever Jesus comes He establishes rest." When we take the yoke of Christ upon us, we find the peace of Christ within us. Let us hurry to find *that* rest!

**Stand at the crossroads and look; ask for the ancient paths,
ask where the good way is, and walk in it, and you will
find rest for your souls (Jer. 6:16).**

Why Does God Delay?

I have learned that *delay* is an often-used word in the disciple's vocabulary. Have you ever wondered why some of your prayers have gone unnoticed, as if heaven had shut up shop? God says, "Therefore will the Lord wait, that he may be gracious unto you" (Isa. 30:18, KJV). How can His waiting result in blessing instead of inconvenience?

Let's note that *time* has a great deal to do with making us holy. The time frame of the natural person is "Now!" But suppose God gave us everything we wanted *now*. Suppose He catered to our every whim. What would happen? For one thing, *praise* would lose its meaning. Praise is born in gratitude, and gratitude is the result of having a need graciously supplied by God. If He gave us immediate satisfaction in everything, He would be treating us no differently than the natural man within us, whose very nature is: "I want satisfaction now!" That's why the old Adam is "unthankful" and, therefore, "unholy" (2 Tim. 3:2, KJV). On the other hand, God sometimes delays His deliverances in order to heighten the spirit of thankfulness and praise within us.

Another thing—God delays because He wants us to value His will for its *own* sake. Amy Carmichael tells of Mimosa, an Indian girl enrolled in her mission school, who later became a believer. She knew little of the Bible, but learned one valuable lesson: "Whatever You do is good." This truth about God sustained her in later trials. When I was younger believer, I rejoiced when God's will coincided with mine. I saw its value strictly from a personal (and selfish) standpoint. Now I know that God has His own purpose, and I must value that will because it is my highest good. It is meritorious for its own sake, not simply because it makes me more comfortable. So I must press on to maturity until I can cheerfully praise the Lord for His will because of what it *is*, not what it does. Like Mimosa, I must "prove [put to the test and find effective] what is that good, and acceptable, and perfect, will of God" (Rom. 12:2, KJV).

I desire to do your will, O my God; your law is within my heart (Ps. 40:8).

How Believers Are Born

How encouraging that God "takes delight in his people" (Ps. 149:4). One of these delights is our spiritual birth. All His children are born in the same way. We are born by His *choice*: "He chose us in him before the creation of the world" (Eph. 1:4). How confirming to know we are neither unwanted nor accidental. God purposed our existence long before the earth was formed. We were also born from His *heart*: "He destined us in love to be his sons" (v. 5, RSV). Love was the spring of His action, the fountainhead of His choice. This means that we are *emotionally* God's as well as theologically His. He didn't choose us by doctrine but by a heart overabounding with love for us.

We were also born by God's *will*: "He destined us . . . according to the purpose of his will" (v. 5, RSV). He wanted us because He loved us and, because He loved us, He chose us to be His.

47

The result is that while we were sinners, God has made us saints; while we were enemies, God has made us His children (Rom. 5:6-10). If we view our spiritual birth as God accepting us, not us accepting Him, we will realize the dignity of being "accepted in the beloved" (Eph. 1:6, KJV). We will appreciate what God said to us through Israel, "I... entered into a covenant with you... and you became mine" (Ezek. 16:8).

Our spiritual rebirth is the triumph of God's will. In 1936 the Nazis premiered a film entitled *The Triumph of the Will,* which attempted to show that Germany's rebirth as a world power was due to the iron will of Adolf Hitler. History has shown us how evil that will was. But God's will is born of goodness. Our conversion is not due to our stirred-up emotions but to the loving selection of the Almighty One. Therefore, we are born to stability. God's character stands behind us: His promises stand beside us, and Calvary stands with us. In an age of momentous changes, we praise God that our reference point never moves. We are God's dear children forever!

He saved us through the washing of rebirth and renewal by the Holy Spirit, whom he poured out on us generously through Jesus Christ (Titus 3:5-6).

First Love Versus Tired Love

Love comes in many forms, but God's word singles out two for special mention: *first* love (Rev. 2:4), and *tired* love (Mic. 6:3). First love is young, immature love, but it is sincere and whole-hearted. It is most often seen in new converts. It blooms profusely. It is sometimes brash, but innocently so. It is totally selfless.

Tired love, on the other hand, is jaded, taken-for-granted love. It is love smothered by rites and rituals which have form but no substance. It lacks both spontaneity and enthusiasm. It is indifferent love. It is the love of discomfort: God is not comfortable with us nor we with Him.

There is no doubt which kind of love God favors. Nor is there any doubt about the hurt He feels when He knows our love for Him is held together by meaningless habits. "O My people, what have I done to you? And how have I wearied you?" (Mic. 6:3, NKJV).

How does first love degenerate into tired love? When our love for God is no longer feeling but *form*. This kind of love is like a motor running on momentum after the power is cut off. It is highly vulnerable to the world's attractions, a believer waiting for backsliding to happen.

Also, love tires when it requires greater effort to maintain than we are willing to make. It has already asked the question, "Is it worth it?" and has answered "no." This means there has been a fundamental change. God is no longer our highest priority, our best Friend, our chief joy. He is still in our lives, but not the sweet delight He once was.

When love descends to this, what can we do? Charles James Fox, the English statesman, said, "When a nation loses its way, it must return to its origins." This can be applied spiritually. When Jacob floundered, God said, "Arise, go up to Bethel, and dwell there" (Gen. 35:1, KJV). Why Bethel? That was where he first met the Lord and covenanted to walk with Him. The cure for tired love is to return to the time when our love for God was as strong as death. There we find Him, and there our hearts are refilled.

I will heal their waywardness and love them freely (Hos. 14:4).

Characteristics of the True Servant

Christianity is essentially a Person, Jesus Christ, and Jesus is essentially a servant. His servantship was not something He assumed just while on earth; He is always a servant (Isa. 52:13). His earthly ministry was not a series of acts for "show" but the expression of Him who in "the very nature" became a servant (Phil. 2:7). He is the epitome of servantship, the model for all His followers who yearn to serve.

The true servant surrenders *pride*. Jesus described Himself as "one who serves," then illustrated what He meant by washing His disciples' feet (Luke 22:27; John 13). He did not allow His equality with the Father to prevent Him from doing a servant's task. Had He done so, he could never have assumed the servant role. Pride is the enemy of servantship because it puts barriers between us and the person in need. Dietrich Bonhoeffer says, "Nobody is too good for the meanest service." Jesus served because He loved His disciples—so much that the Bible says, "he now showed them the full extent of his love" (John 13:1). That's why He became "obedient unto death" for us all.

The true servant identifies with *needy people*. The story of the good Samaritan is Jesus' description of His own servanthood (Luke 10); He is the good Samaritan. The Samaritan left his comfortable place to align himself with a robbed, beaten stranger who had no one to help him. Spiritually, this is what Jesus did for us. Practically, this is how we are to treat the sin-bruised and battered of our society. The theme of the parable is how much one person sacrificed for the welfare of another. The servant doesn't set fees or ask for fringe benefits. He serves because of the intrinsic value of those who are needy.

We must give our hands and feet to Jesus that He might serve through us. Servantship is not an option but a calling, not an extracurricular activity but our very lives.

***Now that I, your Lord and Teacher, have washed your feet,
you also should wash one another's feet (John 13:14).***

Christ
Is Enough

One lad, recently converted, said to his pastor, "I always knew Jesus was necessary, but I didn't know He was enough." We become Christians because we know Jesus is *necessary*; we grow as disciples when we learn He is *enough* for our needs.

This is what Christ's disciples learned. When they first met Him they spent a whole day with Him, scrutinizing Him and taking His measure (John 1:38-39). What did they talk about? Many things, no doubt. But at the end of the day they were satisfied that He was indeed "the Christ" (v. 41). Yet Jesus did not reveal to them all that He was. Even after three years of intimacy, they were still learning about Him.

We accept Christ because we are convinced He is the Savior. But He's a lot more than that! We also need to accept Him as Healer, Companion, Deliverer, Teacher, Master, King, Provider, Comforter, and many other things. A Christian is constantly believing. The Lord continues to reveal Himself to us in new, fresh ways, and with each disclosure He expects a fresh response of trust. Note how often the disciples "believed" on Jesus: after He turned water into wine (2:11); after the feeding of the five thousand (6:69); after His upper room talk (16:29-31); and after His resurrection (20:8,28).

Each time Jesus shows us something new about Himself, He expects us to take Him to be that very thing. This is how He becomes fully sufficient for all our needs. He has as many sides to His personality as we have needs—and infinitely more. His grace is manifold, and so is He (1 Pet. 4:10). Jesus showed His disciples what they needed, then showed them He was the One who could provide it. We must find Jesus adequate as Savior—that's necessary—but we must also find Him sufficient for every challenge on our pilgrim path.

He who did not spare His own Son . . . how shall He not with Him also freely give us all things (Rom. 8:32, NKJV).

The Value
of Affliction

God is the God of efficiency. The crowds said of Jesus, "He has done everything well" (Mark 7:37). This was their testimony of Him who did everything perfectly. God wastes no motions in either creation or redemption. Nor with us. So when God brings affliction, we must look for the value He intends by it.

Job teaches us this. His life evoked many themes, chief of which was the Lord's sovereign right to rule us. Another was suffering and its value. One benefit Job gained through adversity was spiritual refinement. His troubles revealed the true state of his heart, and this exposure was the beginning of his cleansing. There can be no purifying unless there is first revelation. Job's problem was not that he wasn't good, he wasn't good enough. The only way God could raise him to the next level of goodness was to show him how much farther he had to go. As George

MacDonald says, "Job sought justification; he found self-abhorrence." This abhorrence was necessary to his becoming a purified believer.

The immediate work of all adversity is *inward*. Nothing makes us look within more quickly than trouble. Like Job, we start analyzing ourselves, probing for the cause of our difficulty, and this is what God wants. We begin to see our true selves. Self-deception fades before the cold realism of suffering. The Holy Spirit is then able to reveal to us the dark spots of our characters until we cry to Him for help. That's what God did with Job. And Job responded: "My ears had heard of you but now my eyes have seen you. Therefore I despise myself and repent" (Job 42:5-6).

Job's humility at the end of the book is a sharp contrast to his boasts of innocence all through. Seeing what he really was, he humbled himself and came through. Affliction has value! Let's learn it as Job did and praise God for its great benefit.

In faithfulness you have afflicted me (Ps. 119:75).

Greater Things

Jesus said to the would-be disciple, Nathaniel, "Behold an Israelite indeed, in whom is no guile!" (John 1:47, KJV). Surprised, Nathaniel replied, "How do you know me?" Jesus answered, "Before Philip called you, when you were under the fig tree, I saw you" (v. 48, RSV).

Does Jesus see us without guile, that is, sincere? If so, then He is ready to take the next step and show us "greater things" (v. 50). What are these "greater things"? Briefly, a greater awareness of ourselves and a greater awareness of Christ. Christian theology maintains that we cannot know God apart from Jesus. True! Neither can we know ourselves apart from Him. No study of psychology will reveal a better awareness of ourselves than knowing Christ will. He shows us not only what we are, but what we can be (v. 42). "In your light we see light" (Ps. 36:9). In their three-year association with Christ, the disciples learned a great deal about Him. They also learned a great deal about themselves. The same is true of us. Life with Jesus is progressively illuminating; the more we absorb Him the more thoroughly we learn ourselves.

Also, the "greater things" include a better understanding of Christ. More and more He reveals to us the mysteries of His person and challenges us to follow Him more closely. Of course, we can't ever fully know Christ, but, like a mountain climb, each stage with Him leads to another; each view affords a greater breathtaking wonder. A comprehensive view of Christ is what discipleship is all about. To know Him is the chief aim of every disciple. Jesus invites us to reach out for the "greater things" He has promised. This is the crown and glory of life.

I want to know Christ and the power of his resurrection and the fellowship of sharing in his sufferings (Phil. 3:10).

Spiritual Laughter

George MacDonald says, "The heart that is not sure of its God is afraid to laugh in His presence." The Wise Preacher said, "Laughter...is foolish" (Eccl. 2:2). That's because he looked at the total human condition apart from God. *That* laughter is hollow! Like a feeble flame, natural mirth is quickly snuffed out by the harsh realities of human life. Perhaps this kind of laughter becomes, for many, the only opiate against the pain which evil brings.

I'm convinced that spiritual laughter is the only *genuine* laughter. The Jewish exiles burst into hilarity when God delivered them from captivity. They said, "Then was our mouth filled with laughter, and our tongue with singing" (Ps. 126:2, KJV). When? "When the Lord turned again the captivity of Zion" (v. 1). The Jews who left Persia for Jerusalem were conscious that they were witnessing an astonishing miracle—national deliverance after seventy years of captivity.

This kind of laughter—the result of a divine breakthrough in a desperate situation—is the only kind of merriment which carries within it an eternal reality. So let's look carefully at all human frivolity and refuse to be drawn into empty gaiety.

If we haven't learned to laugh spiritually, we have not gone far with God. Ours is a boisterous and humorous faith. Walking with God is a royal road to spiritual entertainment. How else do we respond to the instant healing of a man who had been paralyzed for thirty-eight years? In a second, Jesus made the man's ills appear trite and trivial! Who can help being amused at the astonished emcee, who said to the bridegroom at the wedding reception: "You have saved the best [wine] till now" (John 2:10). Just moments before, there was no wine at all and great embarrassment!

The world laughs at us only to belittle us. But God makes us laugh to show that we are His dear children forever.

To every thing there is a season. . . . a time to laugh" (Eccl. 3:1-4, KJV).

The School of Faith

The disciples asked Jesus to teach them to pray. They never asked Him to teach them to *believe*. Yet Jesus corrected them more for their lack of faith than any of their shortcomings. It is easy to pray but hard to believe. Praying is specific action; faith is an attitude. It is always easier to act than to *be*. Action is the work of a moment; becoming is the work of a lifetime.

How do we learn faith? Three ways, I believe. First, faith is *taught*. This is the textbook, blackboard way of learning it. This is learning it as a concept or a theory. At this stage we understand with our minds, but no further than that.

Second, faith is *caught*. We see someone who lives by faith and see it in practice. We see its fruits, we love its benefits. As yet, however, it is still outside us.

Third, faith is *wrought*. This is where God comes into the picture as our Master Trainer. He puts us in difficult places, like Israel at the Red Sea (Ex. 14:13-18), and makes us sink or swim. We are forced to believe, not through a teacher or an example, but from ourselves until it becomes part of our nature.

The third stage is the most painful time in our walk with God. To trust simply and wait patiently when circumstances shout "Do something!" requires a response different than is customary to human nature. It is a time of proving God to be true or false, able or unable. Concepts are of no help to us here and neither is example. We have to walk through every inch of it until we have proved to ourselves that God is true and faithful. When we "stand still" (by faith) and "see the salvation of the Lord" (by experience), we have learned faith at last (v. 13, KJV). "And when the Israelites saw the great power the Lord displayed against the Egyptians, the people feared the Lord and put their trust in him" (v. 31).

Jesus said to the woman, "Your faith has saved you; go in peace" (Luke 7:50).

The Power
of Small Things

While the Christian life is miraculous, it's also mundane. Paul's stressful situation in Macedonia was not relieved by a heavenly chariot, but by the arrival of a dear friend and colleague, Titus (2 Cor. 7:5-7). Titus brought a heartwarming message of love and concern to Paul from his Christian friends at Corinth. That was all the lift Paul needed.

God's packages are often plainly wrapped. One may be a letter from a friend, another a tract picked up on the seashore, a timely phone call, or even something still more ordinary, like a smile, a handshake, or a kind word. God is the God of the minuscule. Often I've heard Christians say, "I wanted to say something but felt I had so little to offer." A blessing missed because of false humility! Didn't Christ become incarnate as a baby? Didn't Moses part the Red Sea with a shepherd's staff? Didn't Elisha heal Naaman's leprosy because a Jewish slave girl had the courage to speak to her mistress about him?

Let's get rid of the idea that God operates only in the realm of the big and the spectacular. Anything we have can be used by the Lord to minister to others. "Who despises the day of small things?" (Zech. 4:10). Whoever does has a dim, blurred view of God and His methods. His god is a *deus ex machina*, a mechanical god who springs into action in unheard of ways to deliver his people from bad situations. Let's rejoice that it is the "poor in spirit" who find the kingdom (Matt. 5:3). It is not those who are wise, influential, or noble whom God chooses for salvation. It's just the opposite, that we may boast in the Lord, not ourselves (1 Cor. 1:26,31).

Small things becomes a new world for those with eyes of faith. They see a miracle in a blade of grass and deliverance around the next bend of the road. When God is Lord of the ordinary, there is no limit to the ordinary!

We have this treasure in jars of clay to show that this all-surpassing power is from God and not from us (2 Cor. 4:7).

God's Capacity for Suffering

An Indian once said to a Christian missionary: "You degrade God when you say He suffers." How wrong! God can suffer—and does. The heart of Christianity is that He suffered and died for us. The cross is the measure of God's capacity to suffer.

Humans suffer for what we are as well as what we do, but God suffers for things outside Himself. If God existed alone in the universe, He would not suffer; what He does suffer is due to our sin. No one has ever suffered as God has. "Is any suffering like my suffering that was inflicted on me?" (Lam. 1:12). The words are Jeremiah's, but the meaning is God's. His sensitivity to sin is a thousand times keener than ours. His pure holiness makes that sensitivity acute. Also, the strength of His love makes Him more vulnerable to sin's pain. We may sympathize with Peter's hurt when he denied Jesus, but we'll never fully understand what

Jesus felt because Peter denied Him. That pain is beyond us because we don't know the richness of His love or the purity of His holiness.

Isn't it amazing that God wants to heal the very ones who cause His pain? That's why I'm encouraged when He leads me into suffering. He doesn't like to do it, but He must because of His higher purpose. His behavior is never the tyrant, but a Father who weeps right along with my weeping.

I heard a Christian say, "I've suffered so much I could write a book." Perhaps. But not like *His* book, for He has gone far beyond us in suffering. His book is the Bible, which is more than the story of human sin and misery; it is also God's story of heartache over the same thing which causes ours. Happily, His book points forward to the day when suffering and pain will end, both for us and for Him. "He will wipe every tear from their eyes. . . . for the old order of things has passed away (Rev. 21:4).

In all their distress he too was distressed, and the angel of his presence saved them (Isa. 63:9).

The Lord
Delights in You!

God "takes delight in his people" (Ps. 149:4). He does this, of course, generally, but He takes *personal* delight in us as well. Listen to David: "He rescued me because he delighted in me" (18:19). One of the great mysteries of the Bible is why God thinks so much of us. "What is man that you are mindful of him, the son of man that you care for him?" (8:4). Yes, God delights in our existence, the fact that we *are*. Even more, when we walk in His ways, He has *great* delight in us. (37:23)!

Why does God feel such heart warmth over us? One reason is because we provide Him the opportunity to exercise His God-hood. God delights in simply being God to us. Although God never calls Himself the "God of Gabriel," He does refer to Himself as the "God of Abraham...Isaac and...Jacob" (Ex. 3:15). Perhaps it is because we call forth His attributes like mercy, grace, and forgiveness more than angels do.

Another reason God delights in us is because we are destined to become like His Son, Jesus. How much the Father delights in Him! He is the Son whom God loves and of whom He says, "With him I am well pleased" (Matt. 3:17). God never promised angels the high glory of being "conformed to the likeness of his Son" (Rom. 8:29), but He promises that to us! We are the raw material out of which God will create what He highly prizes—the image of His Son. Could God possibly give us any higher honor? David was astounded that God made humans a little lower than angels (Ps. 8:5), and rightly so, but we are destined for a greater glory than that! Shouldn't this fact end all mourning and self-loathing and fill us with God's "eternal encouragement" (2 Thess. 2:16)?

I know that you are pleased with me. . . . In my integrity you uphold me and set me in your presence forever
(Ps. 41:11-12).

The Unknown Path

The Lord sometimes leads us in an unknown way. He said to Joshua, "You have never been this way before" (Josh. 3:4). Israel followed a route to Canaan which was devised especially by God. He did not permit them to take the shortest, quickest road, "the way of the land of Philistines," because it was dangerous (Ex. 13:17, KJV). Often God leads us in strange ways because of dangers which only He sees. Joseph was led to a royal position via a prison, and Jonah reached Nineveh only after a detour through Joppa and the huge fish.

Because of the road's strangeness, God requires trust on our part. Gerhardt Tersteegen wrote: "Let Him lead thee blindfold onwards, love needs not to know. Children whom the Father leadeth ask not where they go." If we comply, He will lead us as carefully and safely as we lead the physically blind. "I will bring the blind by a way that they knew not... I will make darkness light before them, and crooked things straight.... and not forsake them" (Isa. 42:16, KJV). God Himself will be our eyes and our protector, that we might walk safely onward. But we must never complain that God doesn't know where He is leading us (40:27). This is a cruel insult both to God's love and His wisdom.

Because the road is strange, it is easy to miss, and we could wander aimlessly in By-path Meadow, as John Bunyan described it. That's why God "broaden[s] the path beneath me, so that my ankles do not turn" (Ps. 18:36). This is God's grace in action. When we are bewildered and unsure, He will give us *confirming evidences* of His path so we don't "turn." He did this for Eliezer, Abraham's servant, who was sent to Aram to find a wife for Isaac. Confused, Eliezer prayed for guidance and the Lord helped. He said, "As for me, the Lord has led me" (Gen. 24:27). All his strange circumstances finally fell into place.

How heartening to know that *He* knows the way we take (Job 23:10)!

You are my lamp, O Lord; the Lord turns my darkness into light (2 Sam. 22:29).

Our Claim
on God

Before sailing to China as a missionary, Hudson Taylor made a pledge to God: "When I get to China, I shall have no claim on anyone for anything; my only claim will be on God." In this case, Taylor's claim on God was for His blessing on China. Meaning? For the success of his missionary efforts Taylor would have to "move man, through God, by prayer alone." He pressed his claim repeatedly, and God responded with help and power.

Many of our dealings with the Lord will be mysterious to us unless we know what it means to have a claim on Him. When we have a claim on God, we expect Him to fulfill His promises. This means that we can discount circumstances, for often circumstances are diametrically opposite the claim. In Abraham's case, for example, God promised him a son. This promise was Abraham's claim on God. But his circumstances were just the reverse: both his and Sarah's bodies were reproductively "dead" (Heb. 11:12). Circumstances, therefore, said "No!" to God's promise. But Abraham held God's promise as a check to be cashed and, in time, miraculously, Isaac was born.

When we have a claim on God, He reserves the right to decide when and how the claim will be delivered. His claims are all realities, but not dated realities. This means, as with Hudson Taylor and Abraham, that our faith must be kept on continuous alert. We must not doubt the claim! Time may pass, days may become wearisome, the outlook may grow bleaker than ever—but faith must keep up its courage. God is just and, because of His integrity, He will honor all claims upon His word. When the claim is finally granted, joy overflows the receiver's heart. And what a powerful affirmation we receive for our faith! God wants us all to be affirmers of His word!

Let us hold unswervingly to the hope we profess, for he who promised is faithful (Heb. 10:23).

Delighting in God

Here's what David said about *delight*. "Delight yourself in the Lord and he will give you the desires of your heart" (Ps. 37:3). How can we delight in the Lord? Through the eye of discernment. "Your eyes will see the king in his beauty" (Isa. 33:17). To see God in His beauty is to appreciate Him, to enjoy Him, to be thoroughly delighted by Him.

God's Word enables us to see God's beauty. If we see only words in the Bible, we will miss its heart. The Bible is more than verses to be memorized, texts to be pored over, or disciplines to be mastered. It is the self-disclosure of the universe's most glorious Being. He is present on every page in, through, and behind both words and content. There His thoughts and the feelings of His heart are disclosed. When Jesus interpreted the Old Testament to the two disciples on the road to Emmaus, He didn't simply give facts, "He explained to them what was said in all the Scriptures concerning *himself*" (Luke 24:27, emphasis added).

To the spiritually discerning, the Bible is a glory-filled book. The Spirit takes us beneath the surface of Scripture to the God who is the true meaning of everything. He parts the curtain to show us His creative wisdom and caring love. Above all, He shows how He manifested Himself in the person of Jesus, who came to reveal to us everything that God is. When we read of Jesus' agony in Gethsemane and on Calvary, we feel God's agony over our sins; we see His desire to be reconciled to a fallen race.

To read the Bible profitably is to read it discerningly and

immediately. By discerningly I mean to read it with the Spirit's help; by immediately I mean to ask, "Lord, what are You saying to me *now?*" The Spirit is always immediate and so is His work. When we read the Word this way, we'll see the King in His beauty, and our heart will delight in Him. What a glorious way to live, constantly delighting in Him!

Whom have I in heaven but thee? and there is none upon earth that I desire beside thee (Ps. 73:25, KJV).

Christ's Yoke— and Rest

"Take my yoke upon you and learn from me" (Matt. 11:29). The yoke is always Christ's, never ours. To yoke a team of oxen is to put them into service under our authority. We can choose to accept or reject the yoke of Christ, but if we accept it, we cannot choose the place of service. He may want us to plough a rocky furrow, thresh a field of ripe grain, or pull a heavy load. The yoke means: I am harnessed by Christ to serve others. The yoke Jesus wore meant that He was destined for the cross. When oxen are yoked they know it will not mean a day spent in the barn munching hay. To wear Christ's yoke means to feel the drag of the plough in scorching heat. Yet, on the other hand, the yoke of Christ means rest, not despair; inward satisfaction, not emptiness and disillusionment. Jesus used the word "rest" twice in the same passage in which He referred to His yoke (vv. 28-29). I have heard many sermons on this familiar text which emphasized the peace and serenity that Jesus gives, but this peace comes through labor. This tranquility comes through toil!

When Naomi urged Ruth and Orpah to return to their families in Moab, she said, "Go back, each of you, to your mother's home" (Ruth 1:9). Rest in her own home! What mother can say her life is a rest? Yet what other rest can there be for the woman who, in spite of ceaseless caring, finds herself being fulfilled? Jesus expects us to labor for Him, but He assures us that in being yoked for Him, we will find inner peace. The freedom Jesus bought for us on Calvary is not freedom from service. It is freedom from anxiety and care while we serve. Martin Luther said it this way: "A Christian is a perfectly free lord of all, subject to none. A Christian is a perfectly dutiful servant of all, subject to all." Jesus doesn't spare us from the yoke. But He promises that while we bear it, His presence will go with us and He will give us rest.

"This is the rest with which You may cause the weary to rest,"
And "This is the refreshing" (Isa. 28:12, NKJV).

Unlikely Heroes

Who hasn't delighted over the exploits of Bible heroes? But was it as easy as we think? Remember Gideon? He was afraid to lead an army against Midian. God said to him: "Go in this might of yours" (Judg. 6:14, RSV). What might? The might of God's presence. "The Lord is with you, you mighty man of valor" (v. 12, RSV). That's the secret: the Lord is with us!

The great ones of the Bible were not all fearless crusaders. Most of them were timid and fearful, like Gideon. Most of the time God did great works through them, not because of them but in *spite* of them. The disciples are prime examples. After three years of personal on-the-job training under Jesus, they—what? conquered? Just the opposite, they all forsook Him when He was tried as a "criminal." Had not the Spirit come upon them at Pentecost, they would have faded into the dog-eared pages of history. But the Lord was with them. They triumphed and the church was begun.

"The Lord is with you!" God's presence changes a dark night into a promising dawn, turns bitter defeat into a joyous victory. Victory happens because in spite of flimsy faith, slender hope, and little expectation, God Himself becomes the instrument of power, and He topples the forces of Midian.

How often we plead with God to help us, only to discover that He has been helping us right along. Elisha said to his timid servant, "Do not fear, for those who are with us are more than those who are with them" (2 Kings 6:16, NKJV). Help was there, but the timorous aide didn't realize it. In the Boxer Rebellion in China, Hudson Taylor learned this lesson. He said, "I don't trust my faith but my Faithful One." There is never a shortage of help, only a shortage of leaning on God. Once we assimilate the message, "The Lord is with you," all the rest will follow nicely.

I can do all things through Christ who strengthens me (Phil. 4:13, NKJV).

"Give Us Our Daily Bread"

Jesus taught us to pray "Give us today our daily bread" (Matt. 6:11). But what does this mean to us in the affluent West, well-supplied as we are? Our brothers and sisters in the Third

World need this prayer against the stark reality of daily poverty and hunger.

Let's look at the principle Jesus intended in this prayer. It's the principle of *dependency*. In affluence, everything contributes to making us independent of God, and this is destructive to faith. To pray for daily bread is to admit insufficiency, something profoundly distasteful to human pride. This means, then, that the prayer for bread goes to the roots of our spiritual makeup. It challenges the basics of our attitudes and behavior. It holds our Christian experience up to the light and inspects it thoroughly. We may not need literal bread today, well-stocked as our pantries and freezers are, but we certainly need God Himself! To pray for bread is to say, "God, I am totally dependent upon You for everything—food, breath, life, strength, hopes, and salvation." Total dependence is the only basis on which God will deal with us. Anything else is futile posturing.

Another translation of this prayer might be: "Give us today our *necessary* bread." What does this say to our lust to accumulate resources and assets far beyond our needs? What does this do to our faith which, by our constant striving for self-sufficiency, slowly dwindles to nothing? God wants to keep us on a *necessary* string in order that the important qualities of our lives will be exercised and developed, like faith, hope, dependence, humility, and thankfulness. Rees Howells, of the Bible College of Wales, said that *not* to live in dependency upon God is the greatest destroyer of our prayer life. We must be dependent; we must live dependently if we want the benefit of God's vast resources. The beggar life is the royal road to spiritual princeship!

My flesh and my heart may fail, but God is the strength of my heart and my portion forever (Ps. 73:26).

The Son of God with Power

Jesus gives us strength because He is the "Son of God with power" (Rom. 1:4, KJV). When a person dies, he loses all his strength, but when Jesus died He became more powerful. He was "slain to receive power... and strength" (Rev. 5:12, KJV).

As with all of Jesus' qualities, He is strong for us. He does not hoard His strength selfishly but shares it with us. He knows our weaknesses and failures, and when we rely on Him we discover that He "is not weak, but is mighty" in us (2 Cor. 13:3, KJV). He has strength to save us from our sins, to comfort us in sorrow, to deliver us in temptation, and to revive our hearts in distress and despair.

John G. Paton was a missionary in the South Pacific during the nineteenth century who preached the gospel to cannibals. At first the natives didn't like his message and opposed him. One night they searched for him, intending to destroy him, but Paton took refuge in a tall tree. He stayed there all night while his enemies kept looking for him. Later he said that he felt the presence of Jesus so powerfully that night that the incident was one of the most hallowed and joyful of his life. Eventually the islanders began to turn to Christ, and Paton's work expanded greatly. This was because Jesus is the Son of God with power.

Christ's strength is unique because He distributes it to us without being diminished Himself. The most encouraging thought we can think is that Jesus is almighty and He lives in us. If we believe this fact and act upon it, we will be sufficient and adequate for any task He may ever give us. The great men and women of the Bible knew this truth and profited by it—and so can we.

You have armed me with strength for the battle. . . . For by You I can run against a troop, And by my God I can leap over a wall (Ps. 18:39,29, NKJV).

When Is Love Perfect?

God expects us not only to reveal His love, but to reveal it perfectly. "His love is made complete [perfect] in us" (1 John 4:12). When is that love perfect? Love involves two self-actions: self-giving and self-excluding. We cannot love anyone without giving ourselves to that person. "God so loved the world, that he gave his only begotten Son" (John 3:16, KJV). Love is the opposite of other kinds of self-expression (lust, greed) because it is willing to suffer loss and pain for the sake of the loved one. Lust and greed, on the other hand, *inflict* loss and pain. We cannot love others if we put our pleasure above their pain, our gain ahead of their loss. God's love is seen in His willingness to let His Son suffer the pains of Calvary in our stead.

Our love is perfect when it keeps us from attaining self-advancement and gain at the expense of others. Of course we must love ourselves, but we cannot love ourselves and others equally. When there is one apple, perfect love says no to self and yes to my brother. The cross proves we can't love self and others equally. If so, Jesus would never have felt a single nail. But His love was perfect enough to deny Himself in order that His loved ones might live.

Love is perfect when we show God to others. When the Jewish leaders saw the courage of the disciples under fire, they concluded immediately that they "had been with Jesus" (Acts 4:13).

When anything we do reminds others of God, what we have done is perfect. When people say, "So that's what God is like," love has reached the perfect stage.

Tennyson wrote, "We are broken lights of Thee." Partly true. When we love each other perfectly, the world will not see broken lights but the full beam of God's glory!

God is love. Whoever lives in love lives in God, and God in him (1 John 4:16).

Faith's Requirement Is Simple

As I study the "faith" cases of the Gospels, I discover an unexpected simplicity in each. In the case of the helpless man (John 5:1-15), the hemorrhaging woman (Luke 8:42-49), and the blind man (John 9:1-7), I do not see a firm, almost desperate conviction that gripped them, but a childlike expectancy, a tender hope, a simple willingness to let Jesus work. A woman once said to me, "My mother had a simple faith." She meant that her faith was juvenile and unworthy of a mature adult. But this is the very kind of faith that's rewarded in the New Testament. It begins with a simple posture: "I'm willing for God to do whatever He wants, no strings attached." This is the "mustard seed faith" which Jesus said could move mountains.

Once this kind of person trusts God, he expects that one way or another He will work. Expectation is as natural to a believer as fruit is to an apple tree. He has weighed the problem and has come out on the side of God. Expectation is like the leper group, still not healed, but heading off to find the priest to show him that they *were* healed (Luke 17:14). It is more than hope (which every normal human being has); it is conviction that God can do it. It has eliminated such things as uncertainties and, as Christmas Evans said, "It takes God at His word."

Faith must be kept simple. Too many of us say, "I know God can do it, but I don't know if He *will*." However, the requirement of faith has to do with God's ability, not His will. Faith says, "God can" and leaves the option up to God. To go one step farther on our own would be presumption. On the other hand, if God makes His will known, as with Abraham, in that case we must not only believe that He can, but that He will. Unless God reveals His mind, however, the responsibility of faith stops with the simplest of requirements—God can!

He [Abraham] did not waver through unbelief regarding the promise of God, but was strengthened in his faith and gave glory to God (Rom. 4:20).

Faith Means Adequacy

Can a follower of Jesus ever say he is "adequate"? Didn't Paul say so? "I can do all things through Christ who strengthens me" (Phil. 4:13, NKJV). Adequacy is a matter of faith. Faith makes mountains disappear into the sea. Faith multiplies bread and fish and makes them more than ample for a famished multitude (John 6:9). Faith is a great leveler. It shrinks difficulties and expands resources. That's why David could go through a whole "troop" of enemies (Ps. 18:29). By faith he reduced the opposition to nothing.

71

If we doubt that God can help us, it's because we feel the task is more than we can handle, the need greater than our resources. A wife of an unfaithful husband once said to me, "I cannot love my husband anymore." Of course she couldn't—in her own strength. Does God expect us to live life on our reserves? If so, then He is the great "Unnecessary." Faith is living above the natural level, where "cannots" become "will bes." To think insufficiency is to admit that our faith walks on crutches. God is always pleased when we say, "I do believe; help me overcome my unbelief!" (Mark 9:24).

Faith is our bottom-line protection in an insecure world. A band of Syrian soldiers, bent on capturing Elisha, surrounded his house in Dothan. But God sent angel warriors to protect His servant (2 Kings 6:17). These warriors were invisible to all except Elisha, whose faith rendered them visible to him. Simple faith brings help from heaven, but great faith makes it visible! Peace lies in what faith *sees*, not what faith hopes. Syria versus Elisha would have spelled disaster for him, but Syria versus God turned the lopsided confrontation to Elisha's favor. That's adequacy!

A bruised reed He will not break, And smoking flax He will not quench (Isa. 42:3, NKJV). Trust in the Lord forever... for the Lord... is the Rock eternal (26:4).

Immanuel's Land Here and Now

The thought of heaven is encouraging, and the prospect of finally arriving there undergirds our hopes, but God never meant that the prospect of arriving in heaven should deny us of having heaven here and now. I fully appreciate Anne Ross Cousin's beautiful poem:

The sands of time are sinking, The dawn of heaven breaks;
The summer morn I've sighed for, The fair, sweet morn, awakes:
Dark, dark hath been the midnight, But dayspring is at hand,
And glory, glory dwelleth in Immanuel's land.

This hymn expresses the true hope of all believers, but if we must wait until we enter that glorious place to enjoy its fair, sweet morn, we are indeed pitiable people. The grapes of Eshcol can be enjoyed here, in this wilderness. The writer of the Book of Hebrews makes a strong point of this. "There remains, then, a Sabbath-rest for the people of God" (Heb. 4:9). This is not the rest of heaven, for he makes it clear that we are to "make every effort to enter that rest" (v. 11). No one ever enters heaven by one's own efforts, lest the work of Christ has no effect. No! The rest is something heavenly we can enjoy now.

We often make a mistake of making heaven simply a location. It is, of course, but it is more. It is an atmosphere. George MacDonald says, "The only air of the soul, in which it can breathe and live, is the present God and the spirits of the just: that is our heaven, our home, our all-right place." What makes heaven heaven is the presence of God and the carrying out of His will. We can enjoy these now as well as later. Of course heaven is more than a state of mind; it is a relationship with God in which the oneness, joy, and peace of heaven can be experienced everywhere. This is the "rest" which the writer to the Hebrews had in mind. The poorest believers are not those without money, but those who feel they must postpone heaven's joys until they actually arrive there.

You have come to Mount Zion, to the heavenly Jerusalem, the city of the living God (Heb. 12:22).

"Don't Throw Away Your Confidence!"

"Do not throw away your confidence; it will be richly rewarded" (Heb. 10:35). What confidence is this? The confidence to "draw near to God in full assurance of faith" (v. 22). This right to draw near was provided for us by Jesus on Calvary. The drawing near means to claim from God all that Jesus bought for us on the cross. Now it is up to us. If we refuse to profit by His death, then He died in vain for us. To keep from approaching Him is a sign of distrust.

We must be bold if we want to be saved. Salvation is a matter of coming, entering, knocking, asking, and appropriating. No one can be saved who hangs back in doubt, timidity, or false humility. Salvation is there for the taking, freely offered by God the Father. He loves to see us come willingly, and, if we do, He grants us the gift of life. Heaven itself is elated at our coming and rejoices over the lost sheep who has been found.

Yet boldness with God goes beyond mere salvation. There is more in the warehouse of heaven which Jesus bought for us. If we come purposefully and sincerely, we will "receive what he has promised" (v. 36). What an open door! What an abundant inheritance—all that God promised! We mustn't pay attention to Satan's whisperings when he insists, "You've got it all wrong"; "God didn't mean what He said"; "Other people have tried it, haven't they?"; "Look how many prayers have gone unanswered"; and so on. We must adopt Paul's ambition to "press on to take hold of that for which Christ Jesus took hold of me" (Phil. 3:12).

Fight hard against the inclination to quit. We seek rich rewards; therefore, we must press eagerly into the presence of God and lay before Him our needs, ambitions, desires, and longings for the salvation of others. We must not shrink from this; we must press on in faith and determination.

My righteous one will live by faith. And if he shrinks back, I will not be pleased with him (Heb. 10:38).

Peace and Satisfaction —Now!

We must be sure to find our satisfaction in the present time. If we try to sustain ourselves by memories or hopes (exclusively), we'll build certain defeat for today. Jesus properly located His satisfaction when He said to His disciples at Jacob's well in Sychar: "My food [satisfaction]... is to do the will of him who sent me and to finish his work" (John 4:34). The Lord was sustained by a present, immediate joy of doing His Father's will. If we are nostalgic, we will live in the past. If dreamy, we will hope for the future. In either case, we'll miss the timely provision God has for the here and now of everyday life.

In salvation, Jesus saves us *now*. Salvation is not a once-for-all package, delivered once and never renewed. We are not saved yesterday or tomorrow but in one continuous *now*. "He always lives to intercede for [us]" (Heb. 7:25). Christ lives, intercedes, and supplies salvation moment by moment. When tomorrow comes, His salvation will continue to be as effective as it is now.

God always works in the *now*. Today's needs, even this moment's needs, stir His heart to open His storehouse and pour out the supplies. God has nothing to offer me for yesterday except His comfort and nothing for tomorrow except His promise. Wonderful as these are, they do not meet today's needs. We need an ever-present Deliverer for that.

I realize now what is meant by "the healing of the memories." Satan loves to attack us by our past, stirring up bitter, angry feelings by saying, "Just look what he did to you!" Memories can never damage me if I am properly covered by today's salvation. Even more, today's salvation braces me for the problems of tomorrow.

But living the "now" life is not easy. George MacDonald admits that only a few know this kind of bliss—"Those who do not 'look before and after and pine for what is not' but live in the holy carelessness of the eternal *now*." Let's not look backward nor forward for today's peace, but *upward!*

Blessed be the Lord, who daily loadeth us with benefits (Ps. 68:19, KJV).

Childlike Simplicity

Jesus taught that childlikeness is characteristic of members of the kingdom. It is also characteristic of people who know how to pray. The prayers of the childlike are sincere and spontaneous, while the prayers of others often lack simplicity. Simplicity, however, is hard to learn.

We avoid being childlike in prayer because we are afraid of a *no* from God. We think it means rejection. But this is a misunderstanding. Look at Salome's request of Jesus that her sons James and John be given places of honor in the kingdom (Matt. 20:20-24). "[Let] one . . . sit at your right and the other at your left in your kingdom (v. 21). Jesus denied her request. He said, "These places belong to those for whom they have been prepared by my Father" (v. 23). Jesus' wisdom in saying no was seen when word reached the other disciples that the brothers were seeking an advantage. "They were indignant with the two brothers" (v. 24). Jesus' no was an all-encompassing no, a benefit to *all* the disciples. When God says no to our plea, it is a wise no which is better than if He had said yes.

We also avoid childlikeness in prayer because of pride. The opposite of childlikeness is self-sufficiency, a poison in our relationship with God. Of the seven sins He hates, "A proud look" heads the list (Prov. 6:17, KJV). Pride dethrones God and diminishes His power. Even worse, it carries the venom of belligerence. C. S. Lewis says, "Pride creates enmity. Pride *is* enmity." It is no surprise that the father of pride is also the father of murderers and lies, as Jesus called him (John 8:44-45). No wonder then that God prizes childlike simplicity! The childlike person is highly sensitive to his needs. He hastens with his needs to God and pleads for them. And God loves to respond. Childlike people are precious to Him. He receives them and gives them strength.

I am only a little child. . . . give [me] a discerning heart
(1 Kings 3:7,9).

Safe in His Hands

The closeness with which God holds us is vividly described in Isaiah 49:16: "See, I have engraved you on the palms of my hands." This is not only an expression of closeness, but one of responsibility. It's God's way of saying, "I assume permanent responsibility for you."

This is comforting when we realize that our right to be in God's hands is often challenged. Satan, for one, makes fun of it. He said to God, "Does Job fear God for nothing?" (Job 1:9). He followed this with an even more insulting remark, "Stretch out your hand and strike everything he has, and he will surely curse you to your face" (v. 11). In other words, take Job out of Your hands, put him in mine, and see what happens! And because God had long-reaching plans for Job, He temporarily placed him in Satan's grip. But no believer is ever in Satan's hands as far as responsibility is concerned. We may be delivered over to Satan's power for a short-term purpose, but ultimate control rests only with God.

Look at Jesus. God turned Him over to the "hands of sinners" (Matt. 26:45) for crucifixion. Even then God did not relinquish responsibility for Him. When Pilate demanded that Jesus answer him, he said, "Don't you realize I have power either to free you or to crucify you?" (John 19:10). Jesus replied, "You would have no power over me if it were not given to you from above" (v. 11). The Lord was fully aware that His temporary delivery over to the powers of darkness was His Father's doing. Thank God, like Job, He came forth "as gold" on the resurrection morning!

To be engraved on God's hands means immediate awareness. No parts of our bodies are more visible than our hands. However, since God has no body, this must mean we are immediately present in His mind. "Your walls are ever before me" (Isa. 49:16*b*) is God's way of saying, "You are always in my mind and heart." Praise God, He takes full responsibility for us!

Fear not, for I have redeemed you . . . you are mine (Isa. 43:1).

Living Above Circumstances

We must learn how to view our circumstances rightly. We need to know the difference between a true view of circumstances and a false one.

I see the importance of this from Peter's experience on the Sea of Galilee. The disciples were terrified when they saw Jesus walking toward them on the sea. Jesus called, "Take courage! It is I. Don't be afraid" (Matt. 14:27). Peter, convinced it was Jesus and not a ghost, said, "Lord, if it's you, tell me to come to you on the water." Jesus said, "Come" (vv. 28-29).

Peter climbed out of the boat and began to walk toward Jesus. At this point he had the right view of circumstances—he saw the sea as something under the control of Jesus, and he walked upon it. But moments later, his perception changed. He saw the waves swelling up under the wind, and he grew afraid and started to sink. Jesus had to reach out a hand to hold him up. The Lord said, "You of little faith . . . why did you doubt?" (v. 31). Meaning: if you had continued to believe that the circumstances were under My control, you could have walked successfully on the water.

Peter's first look at the waves was true because of his faith. The second, however, was the look of fear and doubt. The difference boiled down to a simple question: Who was in charge, Jesus or the waves?

If we see ourselves at the mercy of our circumstances, we will not see them in the proper light, and we'll grow afraid. Remember the ten messengers who spied out Canaan and brought back a negative report? The giants of Canaan, they said, "are stronger than we are" (Num. 13:31). They saw the giants *in control*. But Joshua and Caleb saw the giants differently. They saw them under God's control, and therefore *food* [bread] for them (Num. 14:9).

Let's not repeat the mistake Peter and the ten spies made: thinking circumstances control our lives! No, no. God controls our lives, and circumstances can become food for our faith!

Though I walk in the midst of trouble, you preserve my life. . . .
The Lord will fulfill his purpose for me (Ps. 138:7-8).

Growing in Christ

The Bible commands us to "grow in the grace and knowledge of our Lord and Savior Jesus Christ" (2 Pet. 3:18). But we grow in Him only to the extent that He grows in us. This means we must give Him more room, more freedom to establish Himself in us. There are four ways in which we grow in Christ.

We must grow *downward*. Like a wintering tree, we must strike our roots deeper into Christ until we are "rooted and built up in him" (Col. 2:7). How does this happen? By developing a relationship with Him in which "[we] may know him better" (Eph. 1:17). This is always our first responsibility—to know Christ and keep on growing in our knowledge of Him.

We must grow *upward*. Paul urges us to "grow up into him who is the Head, that is, Christ" (Eph. 4:15). Jesus is our Savior, but He's also our Ideal. Too many accept Him as Savior, then stop! He gave us life so that He might change our natures to conform to His, "the firstborn among many brothers" (Rom. 8:29). If we're willing, He will supply the power. We must not merely grow but grow toward Him.

We must grow *inward*. Peter explains that faith is something we *add to*. We are to make every effort to add to our faith goodness, knowledge, self-control, perseverence, godliness, brotherly kindness, love (2 Pet. 1:5-9). These are given as a gift from God in salvation's package. The package must be opened and the contents used. A farmer doesn't exult over his seed, he plants it; he knows that seed must be added to. In salvation, God gives us everything we need for godly living, but we must utilize it.

We must grow *outward*. Outward growth means reaching others, becoming like a cedar of Lebanon, so that "Men might dwell again in [our] shade" (Hos. 14:6-7). We become like Joseph, the fruitful vine, whose branches "climb over a wall" (Gen. 49:22). If we are growing in Christ, we'll not be able to resist helping others also to grow. The result? "He told me of a river bright, that flows from Him to me, that I might be, for His delight, a fair and fruitful tree" (Gerhardt Tersteegen).

They will be called oaks of righteousness, a planting of the Lord for the display of his splendor (Isa. 61:3).

The Key to Contentment

Contentment must always be one of our objectives for we cannot survive without it. But we must beware of false contentment, a peace which comes from *surfeit*. Surfeit means I have an overabundance of everything. The Bible is clear that while material things are necessary to life, they are not necessary to contentment. A surfeiter says, "I am satisfied because I have enough." A follower of Jesus says, "Whether or not I have enough, I am satisfied." Paul declares, "I have learned to be content whatever the circumstances" (Phil. 4:11). Besides, a surfeiter is always kidding himself. When asked how much money it takes to satisfy a person, John D. Rockefeller said, "Just a little more."

Contentment is not a question of having enough things but having the *right* thing. When Jesus met the Samaritan woman at the well of Sychar, he found a thoroughly discontented woman. Five husbands and a live-in boyfriend had not met her need for satisfaction. Nothing earthly could have cured her misery. When Jesus said, "Whoever drinks the water I give him will never thirst" (John 4:14), He was telling her that her inner resources were bankrupt and that only in Him could she find the elusive contentment she was seeking.

Jesus didn't offer this unhappy woman money—or even food or water. He offered her something different and enduring— "living water"—His own life (vv. 10-11). It wasn't something made from earth's resources or fashioned by human hands. It was something from Him and of Him. Only He who made us for Himself can fill the inner sanctuary of our hearts with fulfillment. He is the "Contenting One" who brings us quietness and rest (see Ps. 131:2). Francis of Assisi summed it up when he said, "You are wisdom, You are peace, You are beauty, You are eternal life."

Come, all you who are thirsty. . . . Come, buy wine and milk
without money and without cost. . . . listen to me . . . and
your soul will delight in the richest of fare
(Isa. 55:1-2).

When Contentment Flourishes

Contentment starts when we let God take over our lives, but it flourishes when we are conscious of His presence in us. Once we become aware of Him, certain things begin to happen.

First, we discover a joy which transcends *time.* Some people get their satisfaction from the past: soldiers who display their medals, parents who proudly point to the exploits of their children, athletes who cherish their trophies, and so forth. Others are transfixed by the future: "When I finish school," "When I get married," "When I get rich." But God's time is always *now.* He works in the present tense. He bestows peace and satisfaction currently. He offers strength, wisdom, and grace for today's needs. No one is saved yesterday or tomorrow, one is saved now. Jesus "always lives to intercede for [us]" (Heb. 7:25). The truly contented Christian knows that serenity does not hang upon the unreachables of the past or future, but that God is here now—and into the nows of eternity.

Next, we experience a joy which transcends *earthly experiences.* Of course Christians feel sorrow and pain, as well as pleasure. Our God-contentment doesn't immunize us from emotional ups and downs. Contentment is not sedation; but in fact, the very opposite. The God-filled person is more alive than any other kind of person; emotions are richer and more profound. The difference is that the believer is not in bondage to earthly experiences. A Christian couple may enjoy intimacy, but this is not the key to their contentment. This joy comes and goes, but their contentment is rooted in their relationship to Christ. When sorrow strikes, the couple may be deeply torn, but their affliction doesn't destroy their peace. The contentment God gives remains steady in sorrow. His peace fills our hearts and proves stronger than pain. As Jeremiah Burroughs said, contentment is like a lamp that can't be blown out "whatever storms and tempests come." The contented Christian is, like God, contented because He is our sufficiency.

Blessed is the man who makes the Lord his trust [reliance, contentment] (Ps. 40:4).

To Forgive and Be Forgiven Is Healing

Forgiveness takes place when we no longer feel pain from the wrong. We have heard it many times: "I can forgive but not forget." Do we need to forget? Can we blot out of our memories a bitter hurt? If forgiveness is simply forgetting, few of us would ever enjoy forgiveness. The important thing is this: does the memory still bring pain? If so, forgiveness has not healingly taken place.

Look at it God's way. Is He still hurt over our sins? Does He still feel the pain of our rebellion after we accept His mercy in Christ? He says, "I, even I, am he who blots out your transgressions... and remembers your sins no more" (Isa. 43:25). How can God not remember our sins? He remembers them without the pain of the offense. Our sins were redeemed through the cross of Christ and the Father is satisfied. Once forgiveness is given to us through Christ, God no longer feels the offense of our sins. If He did, forgiveness would not be valid. The cross of Christ is valuable! It enables God to be free of our offenses and enables us to be free of guilt.

As God forgives us, we too must forgive others. We must forgive beyond grief. We may still remember the offenses of others, but they need no longer make us hurt. Can we truthfully say we are free from this pain? If so, we then enter into the happiness of Psalm 32, not only of being forgiven, but of being the forgiver!

Two years after her release from the Ravensbruck death camp, Corrie ten Boom returned to that place to speak about God's forgiving love. One who came was a guard who had brutally mistreated the prisoners. Corrie recognized him. After her talk, the man came up to her with hand extended and asked her to forgive him. She fumbled with her purse, praying desperately for God's help. Finally, she offered her hand. The Lord showed her that forgiveness was more than a theory, it was an action—for His sake. Corrie came through, and her worldwide ministry on the love of God was launched.

Be kind and compassionate to one another, forgiving each other, just as in Christ God forgave you (Eph. 4:32).

Make the Vision Large

God has things in store for us beyond our greatest expectations. What desire of our hearts do we yearn to see fulfilled for Him? Do we long to be prayer warriors, students of the Word, winners of souls, persons of faith? We must not be afraid to make the vision large. Then we ask. Asking is important. "It is in the atmosphere of prayer," says Oswald Sanders, "that the Holy Spirit nurtures and develops our faith, or on the other hand, indicates to us that what we desire is contrary to God's will."

The next step is up to the Lord. He may begin by pointing out things in our lives which are not right. We must come up for inspection. His holy eye searches us thoroughly and points out what needs correction. If we respond, He will bring us one step closer to our goal. If not, we stay put until we are ready to make things right.

The process of inspection and correction may go on for some time. The purifying of our desires is not a quick fix, easily arranged. There is pain, as well as sacrifice, involved. God does not fulfill our dreams without the discipline that prepares us for the fulfillment. He gives dreams, not to entertain, but to do His will. In the process of self-awareness, He will show us things about ourselves we may not like. We may even feel like rebelling against Him. But if we face ourselves honestly and claim the power of Christ, we will make progress in conquering the desires of self. This is essential in reaching God's goal.

"There remaineth yet very much land to be possessed" (Josh. 13:1, KJV). As with Israel in Canaan, God has prepared an inheritance for us—the fulfillment of our spiritual dreams. Let's stake our claim by stepping out and believing it will become ours. Spiritual dreams are meant to be realized; the desires of the heart meant to be satisfied. And remember, as others have said, "God is beyond disappointment."

He will fulfill the desire of those who fear Him; He also will hear their cry and save them (Ps. 145:19, NKJV).

Is the Lord
Essential to Us?

When Jesus said "I and the Father are one" (John 10:30), He was expressing theologically His equality with the Father. But practically Jesus was saying, "My Father is as essential to me as my own existence." No one can be one with the Father in the sense of being equal with Him as Jesus was, but we can all be one with Him in the sense of essentiality; He is as essential to us as our own existence. Amy Carmichael, the missionary to India, battled severe loneliness in her earlier years of mission work. She wondered how she could continue. Then God gave her the verse, "None of them that trust in [Me] shall be desolate" (Ps. 34:22, KJV). From that moment to the end of her days, God became her great essential.

When God becomes our essential, other things will become nonessentials. A sign of a growing Christian is the decisiveness with which he divorces himself from nonessentials in favor of the essential. Is the world becoming more or less attractive to me? Do I court popularity, or do I consider it irrelevant in my service for Jesus? Am I more or less inclined to think of the spiritual needs of others? Can I honestly say: "Whom have I in heaven but thee? And there is nothing upon earth that I desire besides thee" (Ps. 73:25, RSV).

When the Lord becomes my essential, I also have the responsibility of being a reflector of His moods and feelings. Nehemiah was grief-stricken when he heard that the walls of Jerusalem were still broken down and the gates ruined by fire (Neh. 1:2). Do I know that grief? The prophet Jeremiah reflected God's various states of mind over rebellious Israel: anger, impatience, sorrow, pity. If I am one with God, I will be one with His longings and feelings for the world. I must be able to feel His grief over sin and yearn to see sinners saved and secure. And when even *one* repents, I should feel His great joy! What a glorious privilege to be one with God, yet what a responsibility!

Be imitators of God, therefore, as dearly loved children and live a life of love, just as Christ loved us (Eph. 5:1-2).

Tested Love

God tests our love continually. That's why Jesus challenged Peter, "Do you truly love me more than these?" (John 21:15). The test of love always lies in the area of comparison "more than these.'" God's jealousy is awakened when our love becomes casual. Christ flared against the church of Ephesus because its love had eroded: "You have forsaken your first love" (Rev. 2:4). The fact that Jesus can suffer hurt shows how deep is His love for us and how aware He is of the possibility of our growing cold.

That's why He puts us to the test. After Jesus' resurrection, Peter and some of the other disciples returned to their old life of fishing. On one occasion, at the Sea of Galilee, He shocked them by appearing on the shore. After breakfast He brought their backsliding into the light: "Do you truly love me more than these?"

Jesus has a huge stake in us, and its success requires our love for Him. Suppose we all cooled toward Him and "went fishing"? What would happen to His mission? Would it fail? Of course not! He will not allow us to fail. That's why He challenges us to keep the embers of our love warm and glowing. If there's the slightest spark, He will fan it. If there's the least hope, He will encourage it. Jesus is a *persistent* Savior!

How did Jesus test Peter's love? By rivalry. Sometimes His rival is a new, appealing attraction. Sometimes it's our own flesh and blood, an "Isaac" who has not yet gone to the altar. Sometimes it's the external world, which allures us as it did Demas. We must surrender these rivals to Jesus as Peter surrendered his fishing. He never fished again. His love for the Lord grew stronger and more triumphant. Tested love makes tougher love. It removes soapy sentimentality about Jesus and drives us into the thick of human life with its pain and sorrow. Tested love always lays down its life for the sheep (John 10:11).

I pray that you, being rooted and established in love, may have power . . . [to] be filled to . . . the fullness of God (Eph. 3:17-19).

Finding Delight in God

On Mount Sinai Moses asked God for a glimpse of God's glory. The Lord replied: "I will cause all my goodness to pass in front of you. . . . for no one may see me and live" (Ex. 33:19-20). Then God showed Moses His goodness. No human being can stand the sight of God's glory; but those who seek Him in prayer will see His *goodness.* Glory creates awe; goodness creates delight. Glory intimidates, but goodness opens our hearts to receive the grace of the Lord.

The primary purpose of prayer is to seek the Lord. Many of our "grocery-list" prayers would be unnecessary if we sought His face first of all. We must get over the idea that prayer is only asking and receiving. Although it certainly is that, it's also much more. It is a means whereby we discover God as a Person. We must search for Him in prayer just as we search for Him in His Word. We search for Him in the exchanges of prayer—our speaking to Him and His speaking to us. In conversing and communing with Him, we perceive His presence and become aware of His moral and spiritual beauty. What an opportunity prayer gives us to know God! Thomas Kelly asks, "Do you long for Him, crave Him? Does every breath you draw breathe a prayer, a praise to Him?" If we can say yes, then we are ready for a vision of the King in His beauty.

Since seeking God makes us aware of His goodness, as Moses discovered, we are led to pray for things that are consistent with His character. Even more, we are brought into conformity with Him until we begin to reflect something of His moral and spiritual winsomeness. When this takes place, we are truly delighting in Him.

Let's seek *Him*, not just His. Let's leave our quiet place not with our arms loaded with bundles but with our hearts full of the goodness of the Lord.

Glory in his holy name; let the hearts of those who seek the Lord rejoice. Look to the Lord and his strength; seek his face always (Ps. 105:3-4).

Heaven's Applause

Daniel was such a dedicated man of God that he won heaven's applause before he died. He was "greatly beloved" (Dan. 10:11, KJV). He was also promised an "inheritance" in eternity (12:13).

Daniel exemplified the principle "As is the work, so shall be the reward." Although this principle is illustrated by Daniel, it is not confined to him. All who are faithful are esteemed by heaven and will receive an eternal inheritance.

Specifically, this reward is promise to the wise. "Those who are wise will shine . . . like the stars forever" (12:3). Who are the wise? They are the Daniels who refuse to live for the honors of this world, but live for Christ. And the Moseses who esteem suffering for the sake of Christ to be greater riches than earthly treasures. And the Pauls who suffer the loss of all things to win Christ. This wisdom is the wisdom of *choice*, a choice made on the basis of eternal, not temporal, values. The "wise" see the invisible world, embrace it, and live for it. They are not wise by the world's standards, but according to heaven they are highly esteemed. So shall their reward be.

The reward is also promised to "those who lead many to righteousness" (v.3). Heaven rewards only *sharers*, not keepers. Those who share themselves to the point of martyrdom will receive a "crown of life" (Rev. 2:10). Those who share their faith and bring others to righteousness will receive a "crown of rejoicing" (1 Thess. 2:19, KJV). Both rewards will be the eternal inheritance of those who, like Jesus, lived their lives for others. Dwight L. Moody's favorite verse was: "The world is passing away, and the lust of it; but he who does the will of God abides forever" (1 John 2:17, NKJV). This echoes the reward which God promise Daniel—"those who lead many to righteousness" will shine like "the stars for ever." There's a reward, and we can win it!

To him who overcomes . . . I will give authority over the nations. . . . I will also give him the morning star (Rev. 2:26,28).

Jesus Guides Us by Love

Jesus guides us not by grudging necessity but concerned love. We learn this from the clothing of the high priest of the Old Testament (Ex. 28). On his chest (over his heart) he wore a pouch of cloth attached by straps to his shoulders. It contained the names of Israel's twelve tribes, and was called the "breast-plate of judgment" (v. 30, KJV)—possibly because it held the stones which the priest used when praying for guidance.

The symbolism, when applied to our High Priest, Jesus, is evident. He intercedes for us on the basis of His moral strength, but when He guides us, He does so on the basis of loving concern. Guidance of any kind is appreciated, but love guidance is the most prized of all.

The gospel's encouraging emphasis is that Jesus not only died for us (wonderful), but that He died *unselfishly* for us (more wonderful!). Like the high priest, He wears our names on His heart in everything He does. If He were a selfish Savior, the Christian faith would have crumbled into the dust of forgetfulness long ago. But He died in love, He arose in love, He intercedes in love, He guides in love, and will return in love. The love motive is the mainspring of Jesus' entire ministry.

When Jesus guides us, He does so perfectly. The three major components of His guidance are wisdom, strength, and love. His wisdom assures that He leads us in the most efficient way possible; His power assures that He leads us through any obstacle; and His love assures that the chief beneficiaries of His guidance will be ourselves. God "demonstrates" His love for us not only in the fact that Christ died for us (Rom. 5:8) but *lives* for us. His main interest in dying was our welfare; His main interest now is our benefit. How can we explain this? We can't! But we can show Him our gratitude as Caleb did by "wholly" following the Lord (Josh. 14:8, KJV).

---

*So he fed them according to the integrity of his heart; and
guided them by the skillfulness of his hands
(Ps. 78:72, KJV).*

The Finest
of the Wheat

How good God is! He longs to give us good things, even the best. He intended this for Israel, but that nation failed the conditions. God lamented, "My people would not listen to me; Israel would not submit to me" (Ps. 81:11). So Israel lost its opportunity. God explained, "If my people would but listen to me... follow my ways, how quickly would I subdue their enemies.... fed with the finest of wheat; with honey from the rock I would satisfy you." In other words, God's best goes to committed people. Once we give Him yielded hearts, He will never leave us unsatisfied. No one anywhere can match this promise.

God gives us the finest of the wheat because what He gives is always designed by His wisdom. His gifts always bless (whereas Satan's "help" always brings ruin), and He gives us the best because His giving is tempered by His holiness. Paul says, "God's kindness leads you toward repentance" (Rom. 2:4). God's graciousness softens our hearts toward *Him* but hardens our hearts toward *sin*. The result of His giving is a richer, holier life.

God endows us with the best because His giving is conditioned by His justice. He never gives more than what He promises in His Word, else He would spoil us. He meets our needs within the limits of His Word. Satan promised Jesus the kingdom, but it was

not his to give. God promises only what He has already author-
ized in His Word. This makes the gift sure and the intention holy.

No one can match God in giving the finest of wheat. His
abounding wisdom, power, kindness, and holiness combine to
provide us with an unbeatable recipe for godly, fulfilled living. All
He asks of us is what He asked of Israel: "Listen to me . . . submit
to me." The condition is simple, the results beyond our highest
hope!

The blessing of the Lord brings wealth, and he adds no
trouble to it (Prov. 10:22).

Talking with God
Face to Face

In a world of estrangement and alienation, intimacy with people we hold dear has become a coveted relationship. God seeks
intimacy with us also. The Lord loved Moses and spoke to him
face to face, as a man speaks "with his friend" (Ex. 33:11). To
talk to God this way means there is no barrier between us. There
was none between God and Moses, such as the Israelites erected
when they worshiped the golden calf. Moses was clean; therefore, he was allowed intimacy with God.

Just as human intimacy means a merging of wills and desires,
intimacy with God means the same. However, God's intimacy is
so delicate that the moment we grieve Him it ceases. God
explained this to Jeremiah when he visited the potter's house
(Jer. 18). The clay the potter was working on the wheel became

"marred" (v. 4), unyielding, so the potter had to start all over again. Our wills are fragile things, and God treats them with tender care. He does not desire to break our wills but to mold them. He longs to shape them according to His pattern, not because He enjoys dominating us but because He yearns for our fellowship. If we want intimacy with God, we must "agree" with Him (Amos 3:3).

Talking face to face with God means sharing mind and heart with Him. He is eager to hear all about us (even though He already knows it) because he loves personal interaction with His friends. This works the other way, also. God shares His heart and mind with us. Prayer is talking *with* God as well as to Him. And so is Bible reading and study. When our conversation becomes a two-way communication, we are talking to God as our friend. Grow in your Christian life until you can call God your best, truest Friend.

A man of many companions may come to ruin, but there is a friend who sticks closer than a brother (Prov. 18:24).

The Redeeming Power of Affliction

When God afflicts us, it is more than the random buffeting which is native to human experience. It's part of His redemptive purposes for us: "I have tested you in the furnace of affliction. For my own sake...I do this" (Isa. 48:10-11). In the great "affliction" psalm (Ps. 34), God keeps His hand firmly upon us in trial: He answers (v. 4), delivers (vv. 4,17,19), hears (vv.

6,15,17), saves (v. 6), surrounds (v. 7), sees (v. 15), comforts (v. 18), keeps (v. 20), and *redeems* (v. 22).

What has redemption to do with affliction? Redemption is dual work: God redeems us from our sins (justification), and He also redeems us from our nature (sanctification). Suffering is the tool God uses to bring the second one about. God made Jesus more fully human by affliction (Heb. 5:7-8); but by the same means He makes us more conformed to the divine image (2 Cor. 4:11; Phil. 3:10). Painful and trying as it is, adversity is God's love in different clothing.

When God afflicts us, He does not treat us like a cruel despot or an uncaring father. He injects His own sympathy into it. "In all their affliction he was afflicted, and the angel of his presence saved them" (Isa. 63:9, KJV). The persecution of the early church by Saul of Tarsus Jesus felt *personally* (Acts 9:4, "Why do you persecute *me*?" emphasis added).

God gives us grace to endure *every* affliction. As afflictions increase, "He giveth more grace" (Jas. 4:6, KJV) to bear them. We may not only see our trials as a means of improving our faith, but count upon a special ministry of the Lord to us in them. So "Consider it pure joy... whenever you face trials of many kinds" (Jas. 1:2). The long-range purpose of God in suffering is illustrated by George Fox, the Quaker, who was persecuted for his faith and was often imprisoned. In spite of the filthy conditions of the jails, Fox said, "I was never in prison that it was not the means of bringing multitudes out of *their* prisons." So God works redemptively in whatever trial He asks us to bear.

God is faithful; he will not let you be tempted [tested] beyond what you can bear (1 Cor. 10:13).

God's Confirming Ministry in Us

One of God's purposes for us is to confirm Jesus in us: "Our testimony about Christ was confirmed in you" (1 Cor. 1:6). How amazing! Ordinary human beings can confirm and substantiate Christ!

God confirms the *gospel* in us. If Jesus died, rose again, and ascended to heaven in privacy, what good would it do? The world needs to be convinced of the reality of the gospel and that reality must be confirmed in us. The German philosopher Friedrich Nietzsche once said, "Show me you are redeemed and I will believe in your Redeemer." Our task as God's people is to demonstrate that the Redeemer redeems, the Shepherd nurtures, and that Calvary is universally effective in cleansing us from the guilt of sin and its destructive actions in our daily living.

God also confirms His *Son* in us. We confirm Jesus by displaying Him. When we accept Him as Savior, we make it possible for His personality to be seen in us. Through the Holy Spirit we are being "transformed into his likeness with ever-increasing glory" (2 Cor. 3:18). We may not notice the change, but others will. China missionary Betty Stam said, "We live so closely with and in Him that others may see that there really is such a person as Jesus because some human proves it by being like Him."

The result of confirming Christ is that as we confirm *Him*, He will confirm *us*. "He will keep you strong to the end, so that you will be blameless on the day of our Lord Jesus Christ" (1 Cor. 1:8). To be confirmed by God means He vindicates our testimony and life to the world. He convinces the world that the Jesus we display is real, and our witness about Him is true. That is, God says "Amen" to our "Amen" about Christ. Is anyone sufficient for these things? Never! But "God, who has called you into the fellowship with his son, is faithful" (v. 9)!

We have this treasure in jars of clay to show that this all-surpassing power is from God and not from us (2 Cor. 4:7).

The Joy of Walking Closely with God

When we live close to God, like Moses, certain results will inevitably follow. For one, God will say of us, "I know you by name" (Ex. 33:12a). How significant! Doesn't God know everyone by name? Yes, but there's a difference between knowing people's names and knowing them *personally*. When God calls us "by name," it means He knows us as friends. On the other hand, there are many people who know God's name but don't know Him. God yearns that we become personally acquainted with Him. He abhors distance between Himself and us—especially the distance of indifference.

Another result of walking closely with God is enjoying His favor. "You have found favor with me" (v. 12b). To find favor with God is to be a source of pleasure of Him. God is pleased with those who possess qualities He approves of, such as godliness. God's grace is for everyone, but only the godly win His favor. Are we living on a "grace" or "favor" level with Him? What an opportunity to delight the heart of the Highest Being in the universe!

A third result of walking closely with God is enjoying His presence. "My Presence will go with you, and I will give you rest" (v. 14). Moses was afraid God would abandon the Israelites because they had worshiped the golden calf, but God assured Moses that for *his* sake, He would lead the nation onward.

Without God, the nation could not have survived. Neither can we without His presence and help. Thankfully, both are promised to those who cling closely to Him. Only there do we find true rest.

As the deer pants for streams of water, so my soul pants for you, O God. My soul thirsts for . . . the living God (Ps. 42:1-2).

Pleasing God

God leaves no doubt about the life-style which pleases Him. "Enoch . . . was commended as one who pleased God" (Heb. 11:5). How? "By faith." This is remarkable when we realize that faith is not something we do but something we *are*. Before faith becomes a spring of action, it must be a source of pleasure to God.

Faith pleases God when it is a way of life with us. It was Enoch's life of faith, not his spasmodic trust, which delighted the Lord. "Enoch walked with God" (Gen. 5: 22,24). His long life of 365 years was one of trusting confidence in the Almighty. God wants our faith to become an ingrained habit. It is no great achievement to run to Him for help in emergencies. This is instinctive of all human beings. God is happy with us when we bring everything to Him, from the minute to the majestic, from highest joys to deepest sorrows.

This kind of intimacy with God is a taste of heaven itself, as illustrated by Enoch: "He was not; for God took him" (v. 24*b*, KJV). This is not a euphemistic way of saying Enoch died but a descriptive way of saying that his life of trust didn't come to an end. He walked into heaven as naturally as someone walks through the door of his home at the end of a day's work.

Faith also pleases God when it becomes our key to ministry. George Muller of Bristol, England, was a man of Enoch-like faith. By faith alone he drew large sums of money from God to feed orphans and to support missionaries throughout the world. Yet his faith was simple and childlike. If he lost a key, he asked God to help him find it and "looked for the answer to prayer." Whether facing urgent needs or simple necessities, Muller had faith. I'm sure God was pleased!

Without faith it is impossible to please Him, for he who comes to God must believe that He is, and that He is a rewarder of those who diligently seek Him (Heb. 11:6, NKJV).

The Key to Finding God's Will

New Christians face a perplexing question. Paul asked it on the Damascus road: "Lord, what do You want me to do?" (Acts 9:6, NKJV). Like Paul, we truly desire to please God and obey Him, so it is natural to inquire of Him what He wants us to do. Throughout our earthly pilgrimage, we'll ask this question of the Lord many times.

And yet, surprisingly, the Bible is more interested in connecting God's will to our *character* than it is to the function we are to perform. What really is God's will for us? "That you should be sanctified [holy]" (1 Thess. 4:3). This takes precedence over other commands. God is more concerned that we learn the road to holiness than the road to Damascus. Here's another: "Give thanks [praise] in all circumstances, for this is God's will for you in Christ Jesus" (5:18). A spirit of praise is of greater importance in God's eyes than finding the right spot in His vineyard of service. Also, remember the great priority of Jesus, "Seek *first* his kingdom and his righteousness" (Matt 6:33, emphasis added). Many of us hear this command wrongly: "Seek first your position in the kingdom," or "Seek first your usefulness to the kingdom." It is simply seek the kingdom itself—God's holy reign in us—and everything else will fall into place.

God emphasizes character above location because the spiritually qualified person is more easily directed to the right location of ministry. Our quest for the right location, therefore, should come though spiritual preparedness rather than natural circumstances. Where we serve should be secondary to how we serve. *What* we are takes precedence over where we are. The spiritually minded person is the best candidate for guidance because he has no priority except God's will, and he is not interested in satisfying his ego needs. He never needs to worry about his next appointment. I have "set the Lord always before me.... You will show me the path of life" (Ps. 16:8,11 NKJV).

I will instruct you and teach you in the way you should go; I will counsel you and watch over you (Ps. 32:8).

The Afflictions of the Righteous

There is one aspect of a disciple's life about which he has a "zero option"—that which has to do with his suffering. The statement, "Many are the afflictions of the righteous" (Ps. 34:19,

KJV), must be understood as necessary and purposeful, not haphazard. In *The Pilgrim's Progress*, John Bunyan said, "The Christian is not at ease very long."

Yet with most of us, affliction is strange and hard to take. We resent and fight it. When God lays us low with a series of tests and trials, we rebel against Him. We know that "all things work together for good" (Rom. 8:28, KJV), yet we greet every suffering with murmurs of complaint.

Let's accept the fact that affliction is inevitable. Even Jesus was not exempt. "He learned obedience from what he suffered and . . . [was] made perfect" (Heb. 5:8-9). How can a perfect person be made "perfect?" The point is, Jesus was not made morally perfect but *humanly* perfect. He could never be more sinless than He was, but He could more fully experience what it meant to be human. By the time he reached Gethsemane, He had tasted every human experience except sin. As a perfect human being, therefore, He became the ideal substitute to atone for the sins of the race.

God's purpose in Jesus' sufferings was to make Him more *human*. His purpose in our sufferings is to make us more like Jesus. The pain of affliction makes true believers trust God more, and this leads to the purification and strengthening of the spirit. He sends affliction with an undeterred purpose—not to make us comfortable but to make us saintly. All affliction is grounded in the goodness of God: "In faithfulness you have afflicted me" (Ps. 119:75). God's treatment comes through His heart, His eye, and His hand. Like a skilled lapidary, He designs to make us a thing of beauty forever. Even in affliction, He does all things well!

The God of all grace, who called you to his eternal glory in Christ, after you have suffered a little while, will himself restore you and make you strong (1 Pet. 5:10).

God Loves Us
Just as We Are

The objects of God's love are people, and He loves us just as we are. Nowhere in the Bible do we read that He loves angels, nor do we read that He loves the physical world. We do read that God loved Mount Zion (Ps. 78:68), but this didn't mean the rocks and soil which covered the hill, but the people who lived there.

God's love is thus appealing because it distinguishes between what we are and what we do. When the young man came to Jesus to ask about eternal life, Jesus "looked at him and loved him" (Mark 10:21). The Lord saw his good qualities, but He also saw the love of money that prevented him from becoming a disciple. In spite of this, Jesus loved him.

God's attitude toward what we *do* varies from delight to condemnation, depending upon what our behavior is; but His feeling toward *us* is as unchanging as His own nature. Evan Roberts, the Welsh revivalist, used to say: "God commends this love to us when there's nothing to commend!" A Sunday School teacher once said to her class: "Be good, children. If you are good, God will love you, but if you are bad, He won't." God forbid! If this were true, God wouldn't love anyone, and our salvation would be only a hopeless dream.

God's love is "everlasting" (Jer. 31:3). Endless love means endless hope. No one can fall so deep in iniquity that he would be beyond the reach of God's love. That's why we must never give up on those who seem hard-hearted toward God. Even though they spurn Him, nothing can quench the changeless love He has for them. Let's be as patient with such people as God is, and love them as He does. Let's rejoice in the assurance of being continuously loved by God, for this is the wellspring of our salvation.

God demonstrates his own love for us in this: While we were still sinners, Christ died for us. How great is the love the Father has lavished on us! (Rom 5:8; 1 John 3:1).

Simple Faith Pleases God

What pleases God? Many things, of course, but most importantly, we please God when we trust Him. "Without faith it is impossible to please God" (Heb. 11:6). Trust is not a contrivance for getting things from Him, it is a way of life. By faith we are saved, but once saved, faith should be the shining glory of our lives. Jesus didn't need to be saved, nor did He have any sins to confess, yet He lived dependently upon His Father. He lived by faith because that's what being human requires. All God's created beings must trust Him simply because of who He is and who they are. We all depend upon Him for life, breath, and existence. Though He was the Son of the Highest, Jesus lived trustingly because He became flesh and lived on the same plane as any human being must.

When we trust in God we are being most creaturely and dependent. Suppose we sin? Then we must trust Him all the more, for now we need cleansing. And if we have specific needs, we must most certainly depend upon Him. All such trust really pleases God.

Trusting God means not depending (ultimately) upon ourselves. What about those who keep telling us, "You must believe in yourself"? Of course, there is a sense in which we need to call upon our own resources, but the true believer always does this in cooperation with, not independent of, God. He is delighted when we say with Paul: "By the grace of God I am what I am" (1 Cor. 15:10).

Some people excuse their disbelief by their frailty. "I can't trust, I am only human!" This is the very opposite of humanity. Not to trust is the most unhuman thing we can do. That's why God begs us to trust and reproaches us when we don't. Trusting the Heavenly Father is simply doing what He created us to do—to be dependent upon Him.

Those who know your name will trust in you, for you, Lord, have never forsaken those who seek you (Ps. 9:10).

The Lord's "Strange Work"

In the Bible, God's works are described in a number of ways: they are "awesome" (Ps. 66:3); "wonderful" (136:4); "marvelous" (139:14); "beautiful" (Eccl. 3:11); "great" (Ps. 111:2); "beyond count" (40:5). But His works are sometimes "strange." "The Lord will rise up . . . to do his work, his strange work, and perform his task, his alien task" (Isa. 28:21).

How can God's work ever be called "strange"? For the Jews, the "strange work" meant that God was about to inflict on them the same kind of defeat they had inflicted on their enemies. This was strange because God sided with their enemies against them. The reason? Because they had made a covenant "with death" and Sheol; that is, they turned to lying and deceiving instead of trusting the living God (v. 15).

The Lord's strange work also means other things. It refers to unexpected and undeserved suffering. "Do not be surprised at the painful trial you are suffering, as though something strange were happening to you" (1 Pet. 4:12). Suffering comes to good (even godly) people. The strangeness is not in the suffering itself but in the use God makes of it. This was Habakkuk's problem: How can God use evil means? God's response to Him was: "The just shall live by his faith" (Hab. 2:4 KJV). That is, trust God whether or not you can explain His inexplicable ways.

God's strange work sometimes refers to His actions which seem at variance with His promises. God gave Abraham a son (Isaac), through whom the promises were to be fulfilled. Yet God asked for that very same son to be offered as a burnt offering on Mount Moriah. This "strange work" can be explained only as a test from God. Would Abraham stay faithful when pushed that far? Abraham believed, Isaac was spared, and God's strange work became an abundant blessing. When God deals strangely with us, He doesn't mean to destroy, only to bless. God calls us to faith, not understanding!

Always giving thanks to God the Father for everything, in the name of our Lord Jesus Christ (Eph. 5:20).

Learning Patience

Patience is such a desirable quality that God calls attention to the person who has it: "You have heard of the perseverence of Job and seen the end intended by the Lord" (Jas. 5:11, NKJV). Patience means, "I will wait for God's timing and not rush." It is a quality God frequently tests by trials (1:3), but trials alone do not grow patience (in fact, trials alone often develop bitterness and resentment). But trials accepted with understanding, and with a determination to remain faithful to God in spite of them, will cause patience to grow deep and strong. The strength of our patience is a gauge of our spiritual maturity.

The opposite of patience is lust. Lust, Oswald Chambers says, is "I must have it *now*." The evil of lust is that it clamors for immediate satisfaction. If gratified, lust counteracts the slow-building work of patience. Therefore, lust must be resolutely denied.

Patience is maturity in the sense that God is mature. He is never rash or hasty. He is long-suffering and self-controlled. To be patient, then, is to be godlike. The patient believer has sure faith that God will work out circumstances for his good and God's glory. Patience is faith at work, faith resting in the wisdom and timing of God. Job is an example of patience though faith because, in spite of his severe trials, he remained steadfast until God's purposes were fulfilled for him.

"Patience is a virtue," says the old adage. Answer: only if it is the result of trusting God and keeping His ways. Patience is not dull indifference to surroundings or passive acceptance of things we can't change. It is a clear conviction that God's will works our eternal good and is willing to wait for God's final results.

Let patience have its perfect work, that you may be perfect and complete, lacking nothing (Jas. 1:4, NKJV).

Reaching Stability

Stability is a mark of maturity because it represents one of the strengths of God's character. Often David referred to God as his Rock: "The rock of my strength, and my refuge, is in God" (Ps.

62:7, KJV). God's rocklike character is really the ground of our faith. What would salvation be if God could not be trusted with His promises?

The opposite of stability—wishy-washiness—God despises. This vacillation is behind all backsliding and was the chief sin of Israel in the wilderness. It was the generation "whose spirit was not faithful to God" (Ps. 78:8, NKJV). In later history, Israel was no better. Hosea rebuked the nation for being "a silly dove, without sense—They call to Egypt, They go to Assyria" (Hos. 7:11, NKJV). The picture is one of complete distraction, driven here and there with no rootage nor stability. Forsaking their Rock, they followed the winds of chance and change.

Satan is called "Apollyon," the "Destroyer." But he is also the great "Upsetter." He loves nothing more than to confuse, shake, and distract us. For this reason the apostle Paul urged believers to be steadfast and established. "The Lord . . . will establish you and guard you from the evil one" (2 Thess. 3:3, NKJV). A shaken disciple is a vulnerable disciple.

There are times when we must set our faces "like a flint" as Jesus did. This means to remain unshaken along the line on which the Lord is leading us. If Jesus had hesitated or deviated on His journey to Calvary, the result would have been ruin. But He whose name is Steadfastness was faithful unto death. Stability must never be an excuse for being a stuck-in-the-mud Christian; on the other hand, it must always be the reason for not deviating from God's clearly revealed will.

My heart is steadfast, O God, my heart is steadfast; I will sing and give praise (Ps. 57:7, NKJV).

Turning Failures into Victories

As Christians, we need to realize that defeat can lead to victory and failure to success. We must not allow failure to stand without challenge, or it may leave us permanently crippled. It takes courage to go back and confess we were wrong, to ask forgiveness, to repay a debt, to return love for evil, and to finish the job Christ gave us, but the victory is well worth it.

Paul suffered a bitter defeat at Lystra on his first missionary tour. At first he enjoyed success, then a crowd of opponents from other towns arrived and aroused the people against him. Stirred with anger, the mob turned on Paul, stoning him and leaving him for dead. But his friends picked him up and carried him out of town, where he recovered. Then he and his colleague Barnabas moved to the next town, Derbe, and preached the gospel.

After a successful mission in Derbe, "They returned to Lystra ... strengthening the disciples" (Acts 14:21-22). The story is told matter-of-factly, but think of the emotions they felt. Back to Lystra, the place where Paul was left for dead? Unthinkable! That spot was Paul's nadir, the place where his enemies could exult, "We've finished him!" But Paul went back and turned his humiliating defeat into a significant victory. Lystra was Timothy's hometown (16:1), and it was probably at that time that Paul first met him. Timothy became Paul's most influential helper and "son in the faith" (1 Tim. 1:2).

Paul left an illustration of a biblical principle: the will of God admits no defeat. If a setback occurs, we return to it, disarm it, and compel it to yield its victory. What painful discipline it takes to return to a failure, but what joy and growth result!

As servants of God we commend ourselves. . . . dying, and yet we live on; beaten, and yet not killed; sorrowful, yet always rejoicing; poor, yet making many rich; having nothing, and yet possessing everything (2 Cor. 6:4,9-10).

The Tyranny of the Urgent

If we allow it, most of our lives will be dominated by urgencies. We live in an urgent world where duties are demanding and schedules show how time controls us. Yet, the urgent life may not be the fruitful life; in fact, it can be the destructive life.

No one needed to be more urgent than Jesus, yet He was never tyrannized by time. True, some of His would-be followers felt the power of the urgent. One man whom Jesus called to follow Him excused himself on the grounds of an urgency: "Lord, first let me go and bury my father" (Luke 9:59). This man made the mistake of exchanging the important for the urgent. He was unaware, as we often are, of the difference between the important and the urgent. A friend once said, "The important never demands; the urgent always demands." The urgent forces itself upon us while the important stands in the wings waiting. That's why the important must be sought until it is finally caught. The man who went home to bury his father was snared on the hook of urgency. Instead, he should have followed Jesus' command and sought the welfare of others.

There are times, of course, when the important becomes urgent (Heb. 3:7-8; 2 Cor. 6:1-2) but we must develop the spiritual wisdom to know when the two combine. In the meantime we must deny meaningless, empty urgencies. To do this, we must have a purpose and a goal. Jesus was carefully attuned to God's will as He moved steadily toward the important matter of His life, the cross. He was urgency free! He was no derelict ship influenced by blowing winds and surging tides. We must choose the "one thing...needful" (Luke 10:42, KJV), God's purpose for us, and press steadily on to its conclusion.

Paul's great fear was that he might be a "castaway" (1 Cor. 9:27, KJV). A castaway is not a deep-dyed sinner, but a believer who majors in nonessentials. "This one thing I do" (Phil 3:13, KJV) was his instinct, and it must be ours.

No one who puts his hand to the plow and looks back is fit for service in the kingdom of God (Luke 9:62).

Content in All Circumstances

Paul shares a valuable lesson, "I have learned to be content whatever the circumstances.... whether well fed or hungry" (Phil. 4:11-12). No one can be composed in adverse circumstances unless one believes God is in control of all things. Job made this clear to his wife when she lashed out at God because of their many troubles. He said to her, "Shall we receive good at the hand of God, and shall we not receive evil?" (Job 2:10, KJV). The core of Job's composure was the conviction that all experiences—whether troubles or blessings—come from God's hand. Why not accept what He sends? Why not trust His wise love and be thankful?

Unfortunately, many of us haven't learned the art of contentment as Job and Paul did. We are slow to see God's wisdom when it leads to *pain*. Our first reaction is denial. This was Peter's response when Jesus announced that He must go to Jerusalem, suffer, and be killed. Peter said, "Never, Lord! This shall never happen to you!" (Matt. 16:22). But Jesus exemplified the right attitude toward suffering when He said the cross was His time to be "glorified" (John 13:31). He knew that the cross had an aftermath, as all suffering does, as the psalmist explains, "I will yet praise him, my Savior and my God" (Ps. 42:11). Jesus praised His Father ahead of time for Calvary, why don't we?

Sometimes we react to our troubles by magnifying them. Some early Hebrew Christians must have done this, because the writer of Hebrews said to them: "You have not yet resisted to the point of shedding your blood" (Heb. 12:4). We can easily assume the martyr pose when we are nowhere near the headsman's block. Compare this with Jesus who faced Calvary never doubting the Father's presence. He often encouraged His followers to "Cheer up!" He reminded them of the Father's power that was available for *them*. No wonder multitudes followed Him!

Though he brings grief, he will show compassion, so great is his unfailing love. For he does not willingly bring affliction or grief to the children of men (Lam. 3:32-33).

God's Amazing Resources

The fascinating thing about God's resources is that they are quite ordinary! Remember the story of Elisha and the widow (2 Kings 4:1-7)? The widow's husband had been one of Elisha's students and now she was widowed and impoverished. She begged for Elisha's help. Elisha asked, "What do you have in your house?" She answered, "Nothing... except a little oil" (v. 2). The prophet then told her to collect as many jars as she could and pour what little oil she had into them. The widow did so. Imagine her surprise when the oil continued to flow until every jar was full.

God began to work at the point of the woman's need, and He met that need with what she already had. He did the multiplying from resources which she had on hand. Isn't it true that the solution to our needs often lies within our own grasp? Of course, God must be in the equation in order to make our resources adequate, but we must release into His hands what we have. This fact is highlighted in the case of the boy who had five loaves and two fish. That slim supply became a feast for thousands. All the lad needed was to hand over his resources to Jesus and trust His multiplying power.

However, God never multiplies anything unless we really need it. Also, we must see the need. The church at Laodicea had all kinds of needs, but they were so blind they couldn't see them. In fact, they boasted that they had no needs at all! They said, "I am rich; I have acquired wealth and do not need a thing" (Rev. 3:17). Result? No blessing from the Lord, only a stern rebuke.

We must recognize our needs if we expect God's help, but we must go beyond bare awareness. We must commit both ourselves and our available resources to Him in the full assurance that His great power will stretch what we have and fill our jars to overflowing. The difference between one jar and many is God!

The poor and needy search for water.... But I the Lord... will make rivers flow on barren heights, and springs within the valleys (Isa. 41:17-18).

The Success Syndrome

We must be careful not to make success the measure of our influence with God. Success is the result of a relationship, not the result of methods. Jesus is not our heavenly cheerleader who rallies support for our programs. He came to live in us, and He will produce the fruit we long for if we abide in Him as the branch abides in the vine.

When He was on the earth, Jesus didn't publicize Himself. The fame that spread abroad because of Him was Holy Spirit fame. It fanned out like wildfire because lives were changed and bodies were healed by the power of the Spirit.

After Pentecost, the apostles, filled with the same Spirit, *became* the news. They did not need advance men, promoters, or advertisers. They didn't buy ads in the *Jerusalem Times*. They gained a hearing because people were convinced by the miracles they performed and the message they preached. This kind of success makes the world jealous. Simon Magus was so jealous of the power of the apostles that he wanted to buy it (Acts 8:18-19)! How sharp the world is! The worldly wise know they can imitate methods, promotions, and publicity. But they don't know that they can't duplicate the power of the Spirit of God. How strange the church is sometimes—it has the One the world doesn't have, yet it often ignores Him to resort to the crude, ineffectual ways of the world to attain success.

Spiritual success is in our relationship with Jesus Christ. Just as He was fruitful because of His relationship with the Father, so we are fruitful in the same way. When we do it Jesus' way, we will be able to say, "I have brought you glory on earth by completing the work you gave me to do" (John 17:4).

We must not allow our power, as Jim Elliot said, "to be dissipated in nonessentials." We must measure our success by the tenacity of our abiding in Christ. According to His formula, abiding is always success.

No branch can bear fruit by itself; it must remain in the vine. Neither can you bear fruit unless you remain in me (John 15:4).

The Unnecessary Burden

Many burdens God puts upon us are *necessary*. There is the burden of God's kingdom: "Seek first his kingdom" (Matt. 6:33). This is a burden we must assume. Also there is the burden of the cross: "If anyone would come after me, he must deny himself and take up his cross and follow me" (Mark 8:34). To take up the cross is to surrender to Jesus and follow Him. This is also necessary. Finally, there is the burden of our brother: "Carry each other's burdens" (Gal. 6:2). These are all necessary burdens, prescribed by God.

On the other hand, there is the *unnecessary* burden. This is the burden we load on ourselves without God's permission. Jesus said, "Do not worry about tomorrow, for tomorrow will worry about itself" (Matt. 6:34). Anxiety about tomorrow's need is a burden God never intended for us to bear. Once we settle our spiritual priorities, we must let the material take care of itself.

Also, we must not load ourselves with anxiety but rather treat all anxiety as an intrusion, and load it instead upon God. "Cast all your anxiety on him because he cares for you" (1 Pet. 5:7). A translation could be, "Cast all your care on Him for you are *His* care." Paul said the same thing in different words, "Do not be anxious about anything, but in everything, by prayer and petition, with thanksgiving, present your requests to God" (Phil. 4:6). The unloading of our unnecessary burdens takes place in prayer. Prayer time should be "transfer time." This is when we slip out from underneath the load and shift it onto the shoulders of God.

God does not intend that a single unnecessary burden should intrude upon our peace or serenity of mind. He intends that we should turn everything over "to him who judges justly" (1 Pet. 2:23). The moment we release our detractors into His hands, we come free from burdens which He never intended us to carry. Instead, He will carry those burdens.

Cast your cares on the Lord and he will sustain you; he will never let the righteous fall (Ps. 55:22).

A Gift
of the Heart

The patriarch Job longed to plead his case before God. He had suffered many distressing afflictions which, in those days, were believed to be God's punishment for sin. Believing himself innocent, Job longed to square accounts with God. Yet he was afraid; "Why do I put myself in jeopardy and take my life in my hands?" (Job 13:14).

The gospel solves Job's need for a go-between. Jesus now approaches God for us; He is the intercessor Job longed for (Job 9:33). God no longer requires us to plead with Him but simply accept His Son. If we do, we are accepted in "the beloved" (Eph. 1:6, KJV); that is, accepted for the sake of the Beloved One who died for us at Calvary.

However, there is another area where we must plead our cause before God. This is the area of *servantship*. The Bible calls this giving "account" (Rom. 14:12). Accountability is the main issue of Jesus' parables about the talents and the pounds (Matt. 25:14-30; Luke 19:11-27). This accountability deals with what God gives us, and what we do with it. On this He is strict!

But rejoice, He is also merciful! He will listen to the voice of the *heart* as well as the will. When the people of Judah gave money from the heart it was accepted by King Jehoash for the redecoration of the temple (2 Kings 12:4). When we serve the Lord from the heart, even though our talents are few and small, God will accept our offering as gladly as did the king. Charlotte Elliott bitterly resented the physical handicap which rendered her incapable of serving God as she longed to do. She voiced her frustration in one of her hymns, "Just As I Am," which God has used as the means of bringing thousands to Christ. God accepted the gift of her heart and made it serve more fruitfully than if she had possessed robust health. Don't fret! God will accept the gift of our heart in the day of His accounting!

Behold, I am coming soon! My reward is with me, and I will give to everyone according to what he had done (Rev. 22:12).

God's Love and Our Beauty

God not only creates beauty, He reveals it. I see this in the description of Israel (Ezek. 16:4-14, RSV), in which we find the steps by which God made a special nation for Himself.

"I . . . saw you" (v. 6).

"I said to you 'Live . . .' " (v. 6).

"I plighted my troth to you" (v. 8).

"I bathed you with water and washed . . . you" (v. 9)

"I decked you with ornaments" (v. 11).

"I put . . . a beautiful crown upon your head" (v. 12).

"You grew exceedingly beautiful. . . . through the splendor which I had bestowed upon you" (vv. 13-14).

The imagery is one of discovery, courtship, and marriage. And what God saw in Israel He sees in us. The beauty He sees in us is both *inherent* and *developed*. "I saw you" implies that, in spite of our fallenness, our latent beauty was evident to Him, but that beauty had to be brought out. Beginning with the command "live," God exerts His power to lift us from one stage of development to another until finally we are crowned with regal splendor. Paul describes this process using other words: we are predestined, called, justified, and glorified (Rom. 8:30). Above all, we are conformed to the image of Christ (v. 29). God deems it worth the effort to strip away the ugly layers of sin which hide our attractiveness. The result is a tribute to His standard of what is holy and desirable. His total transformation of us causes us to burst forth with praise.

No Christian should feel worthless, inferior, or rejected. This is a denial both of the love and power of God. It is also a denial of His definition of beauty. Beyond this, the knowledge that we are prized by the highest Being in the universe lifts our sense of worth to such a point that we not only feel beautiful, we desire to *live* beautifully for Him.

The king is enthralled by your beauty; honor him, for he is your lord. All glorious is the princess within (Ps. 45:11, 13).

Expanding
Our Strength

Spiritual strength is not static but dynamic and varies from person to person, from need to need. It can also be increased. Lovers of God "go from strength to strength" (Ps. 84:7). This increasing power is only for those "whose strength is in [God]" (v. 5). God doesn't bless our strength, He adds His. He said of David, "I have bestowed strength on a warrior" (89:19). He took a young shepherd and led him by stages to become the ruler of His people. First David subdued a lion, then a bear, then Goliath, and finally, all of Israel's enemies. His was a life of expanding strength.

Jesus is Savior, risen Lord, and One in whom "all power in heaven and earth" has been invested. "Mightiness" is now His very name. Best of all, we can tap that strength. Those who wait on Him will renew their strength. They will soar like eagles, run without weariness, walk without fainting (Isa. 40:31).

In *Sacred Stories*, Ruth Tucker describes the tireless evangelistic ministry of Maggie Newton Van Cott in the 1800s. Newspaper reporters marveled at her strength. One wrote, "How she can hold three or four meetings daily, as she has done almost without interruption for the last three years, and not break down, is a wonder, and yet she never feels tired." The answer is easy: She traveled in the greatness of the Lord's strength.

The strength Jesus gives us is total. He enhances not only our physical energy but our wills, also. He increases courage and diminishes fears. Our responsibility is not only to draw down His power, but do it increasingly for even greater works for Him. How gloriously alive we are when we discover we can go on from strength to expanding strength in Him!

I will boast all the more gladly about my weaknesses, so that Christ's power may rest on me. . . . For when I am weak, then I am strong (2 Cor. 12:9-10).

Worthy
of Reward

The Christian life is not one of passive submission but bursting activity full of passionate zeal. God goads us on to worthiness—"worthy of his calling" (2 Thess. 1:11). Just as there is a "reward" for sin, there is a reward for righteousness (Heb. 2:2; 10:35-36).

God rewards us when we serve Him from our hearts. "If you . . . serve him with all your heart . . . then I will send rain" (Deut. 11:13-14). "Heart" servers are those whose interest is God's glory, not theirs. Heart servers are sincere, and, like Dorcas, are "full of good works and charitable deeds" (Acts 9:36, NKJV). This kind of service is praised by both people and God.

God rewards us when we use what we have. "The gift is acceptable according to what one has, not according to what he does not have" (2 Cor. 8:12). There is a pointed message here. God rewards us only for our own gifts, which we activate in His service. Therefore, all pretense is futile. Further, even the use of our own gifts must be from a willing heart (Ex. 25:2). A grudging use of talent loses its reward long before its use is finished.

God rewards us when we respond to the opportunity provided. "To one he gave five talents of money, to another two talents, and to another one talent" (Matt. 25:15). The rewarded ones of this parable were those who used their talents, not merely possessed them. The first two men put them to work "at once"

(v. 16). The "at once" speaks of zeal, diligence, and a good use of time. No wonder the Master said, "Well done, good and faithful servant!" (vv. 21,23).

God rewards us when we do what we can. "She did what she could" (Mark 18:8). Mary did what was in her power. She didn't dream of the impossible or pine for the unreachable. She had only a jar of perfume for Jesus, but the world has never stopped hearing about Mary! Mary teaches us that if we are worthy of reward, we will be amply and gloriously repaid by a grateful Father.

If anyone serves Me, him My Father will honor
(John 12:26, NKJV).

Obeying God
with Delight

In a sense there are two kinds of Christians: those who obey God from *fear* and those who obey Him from *joy*. Hannah Whitall Smith wrote, "There are many Christians who consent to obey God because they are afraid of the consequences of disobedience, but they find no 'delight' in it."

There are many "delightful obeyers" in the Bible. Moses had a rare opportunity to inherit wealth and power in Egypt, but he chose to obey God because "he regarded disgrace for Christ as of greater value than the treasures of Egypt" (Heb. 11:26). Jesus could have remained in heaven, with its splendors and wonders, but He chose the cross of Calvary "for the joy set before Him" (Heb. 12:2). Both Moses and Jesus obeyed God from delight and, in doing so, have shown us the way.

Joyful obedience makes serving God a delight. Fearful obedience is drudgery. Like the priests of Malachi's day, it forces us to say, "What a burden it is!" If we obey God reluctantly, before long we begin to disrespect Him and the obligations He lays upon us. This grievously dishonors God.

In contrast, joyful obedience is free, light service. We go beyond the legal limit and the bare minimum. We are like Mary of Bethany who lavishly poured her costly perfume over Jesus' feet. Lavish obeyers are imitators of God Himself, for He is generous in His love and care for us.

When John G. Paton of Scotland volunteered for mission work in the New Hebrides Islands, his friends warned, "You'll be eaten by cannibals!" But he wasn't! On the contrary, many cannibals gave themselves to Christ. At the first communion service, Paton felt such joy that his heart almost broke "in pieces." He was a delightful obeyer and the result was an overflowing of joy in his heart.

Worship the Lord with gladness; come before him with joyful songs (Ps. 100:2).

Jesus Uses Ordinary Things

Jesus deals with *peripherals*. If he didn't, He could never do any of us any good. He appeared to His disciples one morning after His resurrection and asked them a simple question, "Friends, haven't you any fish?" (John 21:5). Fish was the least of their problems. The worst was disobedience and backsliding.

Peter had denied Him; seven had gone back to their old way of life.

Jesus picked up the thread of the relationship again by referring to an ordinary, mundane problem at hand. He did this with the paralyzed man (John 5:14). He healed him of his helplessness first, then He dealt with the cause of it, his sin. Jesus takes us from where we are to where He wants us to be. For this reason Jesus enters the available door. While He aims for the citadel, the heart, He seldom goes for it first. Jesus, the master human psychologist, knows that a human being is seldom capable of opening the heart's door to someone immediately. That's why He talked to the Samaritan woman about water, not adultery; and why He said to His disciples, "I have yet many things to say unto you, but ye cannot bear them now" (John 16:12, KJV).

And yet Jesus never *stays* in the peripherals. If He did, He would simply be another healer type who swabbed bruises but never transformed hearts. After cooking the early-morning breakfast, He got down to business with His disciples: "Lovest thou me?" (John 21:15-17, KJV). The thorn of denial had to be removed, the poison of rebellion had to be cured. People who trust Christ only as a "Meeter of needs" will eventually fail unless they allow Him to restore the citadel. "Backsliding" is another way of saying, "Lord, help me in my peripherals, but don't come near my heart." Peter was "grieved" when Jesus probed his heart. So are we. The surrender of the citadel is always painful. But joy comes when the King of my heart makes me a feeder of His lambs and a nourisher of His sheep!

Here I am! I stand at the door and knock. If anyone hears my voice and opens the door, I will come in and eat with him, and he with me (Rev. 3:20).

Mini-step Victory

Victory in the Christian life comes gradually. Of course there are sudden conquests and miraculous deliverances, but the majority of our triumphs come in painstaking inches.

This was how God helped Israel. He told Moses: "Little by little I will drive them [the enemy] out before you" (Ex. 23:30). God chose the gradual method not because *He* was weak but because they were. In spiritual warfare, as in military, we must retain what we have conquered, that is, "stand your ground" (Eph. 6:13). A victory is not effective until we are able to turn it into an advantage.

We can't take Satan's darts all at once. Only Jesus could do that and conquer. But we, through God's help, can take those darts in measured sequences and on a miniature scale. The Welsh missionary, Rees Howells, explained that he became a successful intercessor only through a series of individual victories. After one strenuous victory, he said, "The next case was harder." God always leads from smaller to larger tests, from tinier to more significant victories. He gives us "one blessing after another" (John 1:16), meaning strength for each conflict and, when the warfare is really tough, "he gives us more grace" (Jas. 4:6).

We admire the Bible heroes and marvel at their exploits. But remember that those wonders they performed came after many testings in which they learned how to win. Abraham is a case in point: "By faith Abraham, when God tested him, offered Isaac as a sacrifice" (Heb. 11:17). Which sounds as if this was the only test God put Abraham through. But read it this way, "When God *really* tested him!" God had already put Abraham through a number of conflicts, some of which he won, others he lost. Then God laid on him the strongest test of all—the sacrifice of his son. And by God's grace, Abraham triumphed. We must be ready for anything God lays on us; but take heart, He will give us the strength to get through.

The Lord is my rock, my fortress and my deliverer; my God is my rock . . . and I am saved from my enemies (Ps. 18:2-3).

How Love
Expresses Itself

Love has three ways of expressing itself: love as *feeling*, as *action*, and as *life*. All three are found in the Bible and all are genuine expressions of love on different levels.

Love as feeling is an emotional thing. Ruth's love for Naomi, David's love for Jonathan, and Peter's love for Jesus are on this level. This is the infant stage of love, changeable, subject to stress and strain, easily discouraged and just as easily revived. If we love Jesus with our feelings only, our love will be vulnerable.

Love as action is based on such verses as John 3:16, "God so loved . . . that he gave." Certainly love must express itself in action. Mary's anointing of Jesus' feet with costly nard is an example of this kind of love (John 12). The life Jesus gave for us on Calvary is the supreme manifestation of His deep love for us. Love as action is deeper than love as feeling, deep enough to be expressed in acts of sacrificial giving.

The deepest, most powerful expression of love is that of life. When Jesus was on earth, He not only did loving things, He *was* love. He was love to His enemies as well as His friends. He came to "do good," and this do-good love took Him to a cross. A Christian under a Communist regime was beaten for her faith and jailed. She said that when released, she would "go again and tell my friends about the love of Christ." This is character love, the kind which Jesus exemplified. When Christ's love permeates us as yeast permeates dough, we not only feel and express love, we are love. A pastor on vacation visited another church and said, "Before the preacher had said more than a few sentences, I could feel the power of Christ's love in him."

The verbs which describe love in 1 Corinthians 13 are all in the present tense, indicating ongoing action, the kind found in character love. Can we come up to that kind of love right now?

Let us love one another, for love comes from God. Everyone who loves has been born of God and knows God (1 John 4:7).

Crisis Obedience

We must distinguish between spur-of-the-moment obedience to Christ and crisis obedience. Spur-of-the-moment obedience is that which the newly healed demon-possessed man showed when he begged Jesus to allow him to travel with Him (Mark 5:18). That very day he met the Lord, and that day Jesus cured him of his demon possession. Gratefully, the man wanted to accompany his Benefactor from then on. But Jesus, aware that spur-of-the-moment obedience can be well-meaning but fleeting, put him to the test: "Go home to your family and tell them how much the Lord has done for you" (v. 20). And the man went home.

Crisis obedience, on the other hand, comes at the end of a long struggle between us and God. Just before Augustine's conversion he prayed, "How long, how long? Tomorrow and tomorrow? Why not now? Why not in this very hour an end to my uncleanness?" These are the words of a man at the end of his tether. God seemed unmercifully hard on him. But God *knows* us. He wisely brought Augustine to the point where he wanted God more than anything in his life. And at the point, God saved him. Augustine learned a valuable lesson he would always remember: God requires full obedience from those who do business with Him. This is the "obedience unto death" Jesus had to go through to become our Redeemer.

How easy to obey God in painless trifles! We love to obey the Lord if it means recognition and esteem, but who bargains for a cross? Crisis obedience, like Paul's, is born out of rebellion against Him. Paul felt the agony of Christ's conviction. He retaliated with "murderous threats" (Acts 9:1) against the church. Suddenly, on the Damascus road, a flash of light and in a moment Paul surrendered to the Lord. The agony of his new birth only served to strengthen his will to follow Christ afterward.

Let's check our obedience barometer now. Forget yesterday's failures, blot out tomorrow's fears, and concentrate on now, this moment. Can we say, "Thy will be done"?

Be transformed by the renewing of your mind. Then you will be able to test and approve what God's will is (Rom. 12:2).

God's Time

The difference between God's patience and ours is *time*. "One day is with the Lord as a thousand years, and a thousand years as one day" (2 Pet. 3:8, KJV). God's operations are on a vaster scale than ours. What we want in one day, He is content to see done in a thousand years. No wonder we lash out impatiently at

Him! We complain He doesn't answer our prayers. We mean: "You don't answer our prayers in *our* time!" We feel God doesn't fulfill His promises. But He does—in His "fulness of the time" (Gal. 4:4, KJV). His promise to send the Savior was fulfilled in a few thousand years—too tedious for us, but easily within His time reach.

When we consider the difference between our schedule and God's, the wonder is that we see *any* prayers answered! However, we'll never attain peace of mind until we adjust to His time. How? By the simple work of *faith*. One psalmist complained that God hadn't fulfilled His promise to give David an everlasting descendent who would rule forever (Ps. 89). Of course it wasn't fulfilled—then. It was fulfilled when Jesus was born. What the psalmist needed is what we all need—faith. Faith makes us see that our unsolved problems, which cause us so much distress, will eventually come right in God's time frame. If we insist that He solve them now, we provoke His patience. Faith magnifies our time frame to match God's. When we realize that our requests are always in God's "active file," never discarded, we'll be able to trust Him to see matters through. We must not confuse God's patience with hard-heartedness or say, "He no longer cares."

Significantly, one of the best books on prayer is entitled *With Christ in the School of Prayer* by Andrew Murray. The *school* of prayer indicates there are right ways and wrong ways to pray. One right way is accepting God's patience, and when we pray, "Thy will be done" we should also pray, "Thy *time* be done." This will fulfill His Word: "Blessed are all who wait for him!" (Isa. 30:18).

The Lord is not slow in keeping his promise, as some understand slowness. He is patient with you (2 Pet. 3:9).

Taught by the Lord

When Christ's kingdom is established on earth "all your sons will be taught by the Lord" (Isa. 54:13). But this kingdom blessing can be enjoyed *now*. To be taught personally by the Lord is indeed a privilege: "I have not departed from your laws, for you yourself have taught me" (Ps. 119:102)

Who can measure the value of being taught by the Lord? Jesus is our example. When He finished the Sermon on the Mount, the crowds were thrilled with His words "because he taught as one who had authority, and not as their teachers of the law" (Matt. 7:29). Where did Jesus get the truths which set people's hearts afire? From His Father! "You are fairer than the sons of men; Grace is poured upon your lips; Therefore God has blessed You forever" (Ps. 45:2, NKJV). The teachers of the law simply parroted what had been handed down for centuries. Jesus spoke with the freshness of One whose lips the Father had touched with grace. He was personally taught, personally prepared by the Father.

God is still in the business of personally teaching those who desire to learn from Him. How much of our sermonizing is timeworn and motheaten because we pass on what was parroted to us? But when God teaches us His word, how fresh and relevant, how alive and exciting His wonderful truths become! Even more, His personal instruction is slanted toward us so that it meets our individual needs. God does not feed us repetitious maxims. He teaches us what we personally may feed upon and use *every* day. In fact, the great hazard of teaching the Word is that we deal "with the outsides of holy things" as George MacDonald said. We must allow God's teaching to revolutionize us before we try to revolutionize others. The Bible is the radiant, living Word, and we teach it best when, like Jesus, God pours His grace upon our lips. That's being taught by the Lord!

I have treasured the words of his mouth more than my daily bread (Job 23:12).

God Protects Us in Danger

God does not always protect us from danger, but He can protect us *in* danger, and He does it in an unusual way.

For example, when the Egyptians pursued the Israelites in the wilderness, hoping to recapture them and take them back to Egypt as slaves, God sent an angel to stand "between the armies of Egypt and Israel" (Ex. 14:20). The Lord protected His people by standing *between* them and the danger. This buffering principle is explained in Isaiah: "Like birds hovering overhead, the Lord Almighty will shield Jerusalem; he will shield it and deliver it, he will 'pass over' it and will rescue it" (Isa. 31:5). By hovering between Jerusalem and the enemy, God delivered His people.

But this protection in danger is not an automatic right for all God's people. Even Jesus didn't escape the cross. The thousands of Christian martyrs of church history starkly remind us that God allows dangerous situations to exist and even prevail. A higher principle operates here. God's eternal purpose is sometimes served by protecting His people in danger; and sometimes—in ways that are mysterious to us—that purpose is better served by allowing evil to snatch the temporary victory.

How then shall we live? By the "if not" principle of the three Hebrew children who faced Nebuchadnezzar's fiery furnace (Dan. 3). If they were to be thrown into the furnace, they said,

God would save them from it. But if not they would still remain true to God though it meant death. Their vision was *God*, not danger. Whatever their God chose they would accept with calm submission. In their case God did stand between them and the fire and they were saved. "When you walk through the fire, you will not be burned" (Isa. 43:2). The personal presence of the Lord is our safety in danger.

The angel of the Lord encamps around those who fear him, and he delivers them (Ps. 34:7).

The Art of Stillness

Spiritual stillness is an art, and in our age an increasingly difficult one to achieve. Calmness is not stillness, but the result of it. Stillness always has a spiritual dimension to it which involves a certain posture toward God. "Be still, and know that I am God" (Ps. 46:10*a*). Simply soothing our jangled nerves will not produce the stillness we sorely need. But trusting God's greatness and accepting His will without resistance will result in inner peace, the stillness of which the Bible speaks. When Augustine finally came to faith in Christ after a long, bitter battle, he said, "Thou hast touched me and I have been translated into thy peace."

Spiritual stillness is a matter of acceptance. Acceptance is not cowardice nor lethargic laziness but an attitude born of trust in God's ultimate goodness. If we believe right now, this moment, that we are objects of God's care, we will begin to know stillness. That's why a constant fluttering of our spirits amounts to distrust in God. The psalmist said that to be still we must believe in God as "exalted" (v. 10*b*). If we think of Him as a lesser God, who is shaken by circumstances or bowled over by evil actions, we cannot know Him as exalted. The exaltedness of God means He is high, glorious, supreme, all-powerful, all-wise, and all-victorious; yet, at the same time, He is capable of loving us, caring for us, planning for us, and watching over us moment by moment. If we can see God this way, we will relax, become still, and enjoy inward peace. Stillness of heart indicates confidence in God.

When the Boxer Rebellion was at its bloodiest and the missionary movement in China was suffering its worst, missionary leader Hudson Taylor said: "I cannot read, I cannot pray, I can scarcely even think—but I can trust." His life's work was torn to pieces, but he still trusted God and found stillness and peace.

Thou dost keep him in perfect peace, whose mind is stayed on thee . . . for the Lord God is an everlasting rock
(Isa. 26:3-4, RSV).

God's Hidden Resources

The psalmist asked, "Where does my help come from?" And he gave his own answer: "My help comes from the Lord" (Ps. 121:1-2). Certainly the Lord helps His people. The question is "how"?

God helps us from resources which are readily available. Jesus' ministry was sustained by contributions, some from women "out of their own means" (Luke 8:3). These resources were neither invisible nor miraculous. They were gifts of kindness from people who loved Jesus and wanted to share in His work.

God helps us from seemingly meager resources. Jesus fed five thousand people with five loaves and two fish (John 6:8). To a slim supply the Lord added His multiplying power and the need was met. But sometimes the "meager sources miracle" is more personal. Corrie ten Boom's supply of vitamins in the Ravensbruck concentration camp lasted a surprisingly long time, long enough to stretch until the next supply could be obtained. How did it happen? "The Lord's multiplying power," Corrie believed.

Sometimes God supplies our needs out of nothing. When the kings of Israel and Judah marched against Moab in the days of Elisha, they ran out of water (2 Kings 3). They requested Elisha's help. The Lord told them to dig ditches in the valley. The next morning, without wind or rain, the valley was flooded with water (v. 20). By means which only the Lord can summon, their need was met. And He called this miracle "easy" (v. 18)!

God is limited neither by means nor the lack of means. His method may be unpredictable, but His faithfulness never is. Are your means insignificant? God can use any means to help His children in distress.

God will meet all your needs according to his glorious riches in Christ Jesus (Phil. 4:19).

The Road We Travel

Each of us has a choice of paths, ours or God's. Jeremiah urges: "Ask for the ancient paths . . . where the good way is, and walk in it" (Jer. 6:16). Jeremiah begs us to find God's road and walk it with Him; then we "shall find rest for [our] souls."

A striking feature of God's road is that it is highly individual and personal. He led Israel in the wilderness "where there is no way" (Ps. 107:40, KJV). That is, there was no clear, convenient road between Egypt and Israel's destination in Canaan. So God had to *make* a way for His people. That's what He does for us. Of course, all God's paths have the basic essentials. John Bunyan made this clear in *The Pilgrim's Progress*: every pilgrim had to come via the cross and the empty tomb. But the other experiences—the Slough of Despond, the Delectable Mountains, etc. —are permitted by God according to our individual need.

All roads lead somewhere, and God's roads are no exception. Ultimately, they lead us to heaven. However, they are designed to get us there not the quickest way, nor the most comfortable, but the most educated way possible. God is interested not only in our arriving, but our journey en route. Sure, He wants us to reach the Celestial City, but He wants us there *prepared*. So the road may meander, may be dangerous, may be tedious, and always requires of us firm commitment and a faithful step of obedience. Nevertheless, He leads us purposefully as He did Israel: "God led you all the way. . . . to humble you and test you, to know what was in your heart" (Deut. 8:2, NKJV). The ruggedness of the road is aimed at exposing our weakness in order that we might turn those weaknesses into strengths.

But God always helps! "You will show me the path of life [that's the present journey]; In Your presence is fullness of joy [for the journey]; At Your right hand are pleasures forevermore [for the journey]" (Ps. 16:11, NKJV). God hedges the road with heavenly joys *now*!

You guide me with your counsel, and afterward you will take me into glory (Ps. 73:24).

God's Stretching Power

God not only has inherent power (Ps. 62:11), He has the power to stretch it. Solomon said God had a "great name...[a] mighty hand and...[an] outstretched arm" (2 Chron. 6:32). God's outstretched arm means He has the capability of adding something to something ordinary.

The miracles of the Bible are evidences of God's stretching power. The widow's oil and flour were stretched from the severest time of famine to the coming of the rain (1 Kings 17:14). As in all miracles, this providential supply was not the result of human wisdom or foresight but of God's stretching power. The same thing happened in multiplying the bread and the fish (John 6:1-13). Jesus increased the quantity of food without diminishing its quality.

God stretches Himself in various ways. Take His presence, for example. He stretches out His presence with us "always" (Matt. 28:20). This is possible because He fills all time and space. God also stretches out His *power* (Phil. 4:13). Paul did not say he could do something (a nonstretched-out word), but *everything* (a stretched-out word) through Christ. God stretches out His grace. "God is able to make all grace abound to you" (2 Cor. 9:8) so we never lack anything. To lack nothing means to be on the receiving end of God's train of supplies. Paul emphasized this in his word to the Philippians: "God will meet all your needs according to his glorious riches in Christ Jesus" (4:19). God's promise is directed related to His ability. How much does He have to give? According to His riches in glory. That's super adequacy; that's grace abounding.

William Carey's mode of operating was: "Attempt great things for God; expect great things from God." Carey found that the principle worked. But it worked only because his God—and ours—is a God with stretching power!

God has spoken once, Twice have I heard this: That power belongs to God (Ps. 62:11, NKJV).

God's Promises, Our Rights

David highlights a need of all believers: "My soul, wait thou only upon God; for my expectation is from him" (Ps. 62:5, KJV). My wife was so impressed with these words that she printed them on a small card and mounted it above the kitchen sink. Every day I am reminded that "my expectation is from him."

This expectation is undergirded by the fact that God's promises are rights which He offers us. These rights are inherent in our relationship with Him. He has given us "his very great and precious promises" (2 Pet. 1:4). He puts these rights at our disposal, indeed, "everything we need for life and godliness" (v. 3). The rights enable us to gain access to God, and they give us the authority to draw from Him all we need to live on a high spiritual plane. This is what David meant when he prayed: "Answer me when I call, O God of my right!" (Ps. 4:1, RSV). God not only gives us the right in the first place, He also assures the enactment of that right when we need it. Like David, we present to God our rights in prayer.

Does this mean that every promise in the Bible is our right? Only those which apply to our need. Example: "Come to me, all you who are weary and burdened, and I will give you rest" (Matt. 11:28). If I come, is Jesus obliged to give me rest? Of course, otherwise none of us could be assured of our salvation (1 John 5:12-13).

Promises which have a *local* application are different. When Hezekiah prayed for healing, God said to him, "I have heard your prayer and seen your tears; I will heal you" (2 Kings 20:5). Can anyone claim this promise? Not unless the Holy Spirit specifically allows it to be claimed. Only then does this kind of promise become our right, and so we may claim our "expectation from him." Let's search the Word of God's "great and precious promises" that we may participate in His blessing!

Hear my voice when I call, O Lord; be merciful to me and answer me (Ps. 27:7).

What We Can Do to Please God Most

What pleases God the most? Is He pleased when we win souls? When we pray? When we praise? All these things truly delight Him, but the quality in us which fills Him with highest joy is when we *believe* Him.

Wealth, social standing, learning, religion—none of these things influence God. Faith always does. It is the link with Him that releases His almighty power. When Jesus found faith flickering and tentative, He welcomed and encouraged it. He said to the father of the demon-possessed boy, "Everything is possible for him who believes" (Mark 9:23). The man replied, "I do believe; help me to overcome my unbelief" (v. 24). Jesus rewarded the man's struggling faith by healing his son.

Christ's most important work with His disciples was bringing them to faith in Him. Sometimes their faith was strong (as when

137

they cast out demons in His name, Luke 10:17); and sometimes it was weak (as when Peter began to sink on the Sea of Galilee, and Jesus had to say, "Why did you doubt?" Matt. 14:31). Finally, at the last supper, the disciples said to Him, "[We] believe that you came from God." And Jesus responded joyfully, "You believe at last!" (John 16:30-31). It was the most precious gift they could have given Him.

Jesus looks for us to believe because it is the door through which He blesses us. He cannot save anyone without faith, neither can He bless without faith. He cannot answer our prayers unless there is faith. As Merv Rosell says, "Faith is saying 'Amen' to God."

Jesus looks for faith in us because it creates a relationship built on friendship. Doubt dissolves into trust. We no longer question but take Him at His word. We grant Him high honor when we accept who He is and commit our destiny to Him. And when He accepts and saves us, we are fulfilled.

Whoever believes in me, as the Scripture has said, streams of living water will flow from within him (John 7:38).

The Practice of Humility

Humility is not something to believe in, it is something to practice. Thomas à Kempis wrote; "Jesus has many who love His kingdom...but few who bear His cross...many admire His miracles, but few follow Him in the humiliation of His cross." We all know how to share Christ's victories, but do we know how to share His humility? Jesus "humbled himself" (Phil 2:8). This means He chose to think "humbly" and live "humbly." Those who follow Him will have the same humble mind.

How do we know that we are truly humble? When we can be humiliated without being filled with shame, but rather praise, for the truly humble person is dead to humiliation. In this he is like Jesus, who was really humiliated, yet felt no shame. A humble person is forgiving and gracious toward those who have fallen into disgrace. He recognizes that he is capable of any of the sins which have brought others shame—therefore he is kind. A humble person is modest about spiritual attainments and does not publicize them. The only exception to this is when God prompts him to share these victories with others to encourage or enlighten them. But even this is always for God's glory!

A humble person accepts what God sends without murmuring or rebelling. To complain about God's treatment is to say, "I'm too good for God to treat me like this." Rather, we should say, "Make it profitable to me, Lord, since I deserve nothing of Your grace."

A humble person trusts God for promotion and advancement. He never looks to others for these things because human beings are incapable of pure justice. God, however, can use even *unjust* men to promote His children when He so determines. A humble person is a candidate for blessing. "God opposes the proud but gives grace to the humble" (Jas. 4:6). John Bunyan wrote: "He that is down needs fear no fall; He that is low, no pride; He that is humble ever shall Have God to be his guide." Humility is not the path to misery but to divine power. The most humble are the most favored by God.

Humility and the fear of the Lord bring wealth and honor and life (Prov. 22:4).

Why God Puts Us to the Test

Do you wonder why God tests His people so much? Didn't Job ponder the same thing thousands of years ago? "What is man... that you examine him every morning and test him every moment?" (Job 7:17-18). Perhaps Job answered his own question: "You will long for the creature your hands have made" (14:15). God tries us because He loves us, and trial is a way of training us to be more acceptable to Him.

Remember, all God's children undergo testing. "Endure hardship as discipline; God is treating you as sons. For what son is not disciplined by his father?" (Heb. 12:7). For God not to test us would mean He disowns us, that He casts us off as unworthy of His time and attention. This would mean, in the words of Oswald Chambers, to be "beneath contempt." God cherishes us, and whatever time He spends improving us He considers well spent.

God always tests us on things we love. This makes the test more valuable. He said to Abraham, "Take your son, your only son, Isaac, whom you love, and... sacrifice him" (Gen. 22:2). If Abraham had hated Isaac, God's demand would not have been testworthy. But loving Isaac as he did, and hearing God's command to offer him as a sacrifice, proved to be a painful but meaningful test. Dietrich Bonhoeffer says, "[God] had come between the father of faith and the child of promise." God always comes between us and the one (or thing) we love.

Keep in mind, however, that God never comes between us and our loved ones to *deprive* us. When He saw that Abraham was willing to yield Isaac, the test was satisfactorily completed and God gave him back the son he loved. God's tests are to purify, not deprive. He demands that everything we love must be cleansed by consecrating them to Him that He might return them blessed and sanctified. When God asks for *your* Isaac, remember Abraham and obey!

Our fathers disciplined us for a little while as they thought best; but God disciplines us for our good, that we may share in his holiness (Heb. 12:10).

Life's Highest Glory— Jesus' Style

The nearer Jesus drew to His cross, the more He talked about being "glorified." For Him, glorification was simply dying. When He said, "Now is the Son of Man glorified" (John 13:31), He wasn't thinking about crowns, honors, royal vestments, praises, or anything of that kind. He had just been betrayed by Judas. He was just an hour or so away from His agony in Gethsemane and a few hours from Pilate's jeering soldiers and their brutal crucifixion. Yet he announced His glorification!

When *we* think of self-glory, we think of the reverse! Imagine a pyramid. The apex of the pyramid is the highest point of the whole structure. This is how we ordinarily think of self-glory. We are above all others, we are the highest, we are supreme. But if we invert the pyramid so that the apex is now the lowest point and everything else above it, this would be the way Jesus thought of His glory. He was at the peak when He washed His disciples' feet, when He was betrayed by one of His disciples, when He received the nails which were intended for us.

We need to reconstruct our view of glory. We must wash out of its meaning all that the world and self would demand and see it from Jesus' standpoint. It is not prominence or popularity but bathing a leper's ulcerous leg, mowing a sick neighbor's lawn, visiting a shut-in or a hospital patient, baby-sitting so a friend can attend Bible class, bringing a lost one back to the fold. To lose our life is to find it again—fulfilled. That's what Jesus said. That's what Jesus *did*.

A modern example of laying down one's life is Dietrich Bonhoeffer. Bonhoeffer took a stand against Hitler's persecution of the church, even Hitler himself, and was jailed for it. Later, as he was led to his execution, he said, "This is the end—for me, the beginning of life." Bonhoeffer taught us how glory comes; it comes in the laying down of our lives for others.

The reason my Father loves me is that I lay down my life—only to take it up again (John 10:17).

The Rest Which Jesus Offers

Jesus promises us rest, and indeed He is himself our ultimate rest. "Come to me, all you who are weary and burdened, and I will give you rest" (Matt. 11:28). These words follow Jesus' statement that spiritual wisdom is not given the wise and learned, but to children (v. 25). No rest is promised the proud and the unrepentant. But where there is humble, childlikeness of spirit, Jesus assures "rest for [our] souls" (v. 29).

What is rest and how do we obtain it? The Lord says, "Take my yoke upon you" (v. 29a). This is not the yoke which Jesus gives, but the one He Himself wears. He means: "Share the yoke I am now bearing." What yoke is that? The Father's will. He bent to the yoke of obedience to the Father. Peace and rest come to us as they came to Him, from the Father's yoke. He said, "Learn from me that I am meek and humble in heart and [having learned that] you will find refreshment for your souls" (v. 29, author).

This is the rest Jesus enjoyed. We may have it also. Look at Christ: whoever felt greater pressure than He? Yet He always had peace. When we obey God in childlike humility, we will experience what Jesus did—comfort under pressure, peace amid strenuous responsibility. He said His yoke was "comfortable" and "easy." Comfortable, when the sweat poured from Him in Gethsemane? Comfortable, when the yoke led Him to Pilate's court, the scourging, and finally the cross? Was all that comfortable? Yes, because the yoke was the Father's will, and in that will Jesus found joy. The most restless, discontented people are those who live to serve themselves. The self's load is neither easy nor light but burdensome and laborious. An old Quaker prayer says: "Help me to live this day quietly, easily; to lean upon thy great strength trustfully, restfully; to wait for the unfolding of Thy will patiently, serenely; to meet others peacefully, joyously; to face tomorrow confidently, courageously."

I have told you these things so that in me you may have peace. In this world you will have trouble. But take heart! I have overcome the world (John 16:33).

The Art of Relying on God

A sign of mature discipleship is learning to rely on God. Relying on God is highly efficient—God seeks reliers on Him and He blesses those who do so. King Asa of Judah is our example here.

When he faced a well-armed Ethiopian army he cried to God: "Lord, it is nothing for You to help... help us, O Lord our God, for we rest [rely] on You" (2 Chron. 14:11, NKJV). That desperate cry did not go unheeded. The Ethiopians were "broken before the Lord and His army" (v. 13, NKJV).

But notice that relying on God does not preempt the need for personal involvement. Asa fought the Ethiopians, even though it was the Lord who gave victory. Reliance means making God the bottom line of our appeal. We do what must be done but leave the outcome to Him. Or sometimes, *not* knowing what to do, we plead the touching words of Jehoshaphat: "We do not know what to do, but our eyes are upon you" (2 Chron. 20:12).

God is not pleased when we rely on lesser things or persons. Note Asa again. He later placed his trust in a treaty with Syria to pacify that country and make it friendly to Judah (2 Chron. 16:1-7). But Hanani the prophet rebuked the king: "Because you relied on the king of Aram and not on the Lord your God, the army of the king of Aram has escaped from your hand" (v. 7). Asa's problem was relying on an *agent* instead of the Lord Himself.

When loved ones become ill, our reliance must be on God, even though He uses physicians to help. He holds the issues of life and death. When Satan opposes us and seeks to discredit the gospel we preach, we must not use, as F. J. Huegel says, "a toy pistol" but rely on the power of the risen Christ. When A. B. Simpson found life "dark and withered," he heard a choir sing, "My Jesus is a Lord of lords, no one can work like Him." Simpson took Jesus as *his* Lord of lords and found uplift and strength in Christ reliance.

The eyes of the Lord range throughout the earth to strengthen those whose hearts are fully committed to him (2 Chron. 16:9).

The "Shaking" of God

God's purpose for us is to bring us to the place where we are not shaken. The person who walks uprightly, He says, will "never be shaken" (Ps. 15:5). Because David always set God before him, he had a sense of security and peace and could say "I will not be shaken" (16:8). And yet, strangely enough, God brings us to this place of unshakenness by *shaking* us! Job complained bitterly, "He also has taken me by my neck, and shaken me to pieces" (Job 16:12, NKJV). And Jeremiah testified, "All my bones tremble. I am like a drunken man" (Jer. 23:9).

God shakes all things—the earth, nations, and even His people (Ps. 46:2; Ezek. 31:16). But the reason for these shakings is good and right. He shakes us as an Oriental farmer shakes his harvest, to separate the grain from the chaff. He shakes us as a miner shakes his sieve to separate the grit from the gold. His purpose? "So that what cannot be shaken may remain" (Heb. 12:27).

Our lives are accumulations. We accumulate things which are both good for us and not so good. We gather attitudes which, if left to ripen, would destroy our walk with Him. We collect habits which discourage healthy spiritual vitality. We amass prejudices, resentments, painful memories, and sometimes outright disobedience. So we need to be shaken occasionally, that the things which are unshaken—the fruit of the Spirit—may remain.

God shakes us in order that the things of the world may *not*. We must not be "shaken in mind, or be troubled" as the Thessalonians were by events surrounding them (2 Thess. 2:2, KJV). We must not be shaken by Satan, heresy, or the faulty practices of others. We must be like David who trusted God as his Defender and could say: "He is my fortress, I will never be shaken" (Ps. 62:2). God's shakings we can endure, for they will lead to good. And may He save us from the shakings of others!

145

God is in the midst of her, she shall not be moved; God shall help her, just at the break of dawn (Ps. 46:5, NKJV).

"We Are Weak But He Is Strong"

Sunday School children sing these words gustily without understanding the meaning. But they are true! Jesus is portrayed everywhere in the Bible as strong. Even though He was crucified in weakness, that weakness was only momentary, for He arose triumphantly, strongly, three days later.

Jesus is not strong only for Himself, He is strong for us. He is a sharer, not hoarder of His might. Paul said, "He [Christ] is not weak...but is powerful in you" (2 Cor. 13:3, RSV). Though we struggle against sin and weakness, we have access to His strength which enables us to "be strong in the Lord, and in the power of his might" (Eph. 6:10, KJV). Trusting any other kind of strength, we are bound to fail.

Jesus is quite clear about what He wants His strength to do for us. He doesn't strengthen us to make us materially rich, powerful, or even comfortable—but to make us servant-like. That's where His strength took Him, and He will treat us no differently than He treated Himself. Paul said as much to the Corinthians, "By God's power we will live with him [Christ] to serve you" (2 Cor. 13:4). Jesus imparted strength to Paul to serve the Corinthians just as He Himself was strong to become the Servant of all.

Jesus gives us the advantage of His strength. We must not miss it! I once said to a woman who was deeply mired in marital problems, "Lay hold of Christ and let Him help you." She replied, "Don't bother me with that! Christ is God and I'm only human!" She missed the point completely. It is because of our very weakness that we can be made strong in Christ. In fact, weakness is a condition for receiving His strength. It is not the *strong* who win, but the weak who become strong in Him.

[Their] weakness was turned to strength; and [they] became powerful in battle (Heb. 11:34).

Tightfisted Christians

Should Christians ever be tightfisted? Absolutely! Without a tightfisted grip on certain things, we'd be faltering disciples indeed.

We must be tightfisted about the *Bible*. Moses was firm on this: "Bind them [God's teachings] as a sign on your hand" (Deut 6:8, NKJV). Such tenacity! The psalmist was even more precise: "I have hidden your word in my heart" (Ps. 119:11). Meaning: the Word of God is not an adjunct to my life, it is my life itself.

We must be tightfisted about *faith*. "Without faith it is impossible to please God" (Heb. 11:6). What a precious commodity! If I lose my grip on faith and trust the vagaries of chance, what hope would I have?

We must be tightfisted about *hope*. We dare not discard it. "Do not throw away your confidence; it will be richly rewarded" (Heb. 10:35). Hope expects God to fulfill His Word, and without that hopeful assurance it would be futile indeed to go with Him.

We must be tightfisted about *patience*. Jesus said, "In your patience possess your souls" (Luke 21:19, NKJV). The Bible word for *patience* means more than the lack of irritability. It means to endure firmly and steadfastly. This kind of inner quality not only keeps us on even keel, it pleases and honors God. It says: "I trust You no matter what the circumstances; I know You will see me through." Patience is a silent salute to the faithfulness of God.

However, let's not be tightfisted about the wrong things. Jesus had severe words for the man who wouldn't invest his talent (Matt. 25:18), for the church which wouldn't share its wealth (Rev. 3:17), and the man who wouldn't deny himself to follow Him (Luke 14:26). Jesus Himself was anything but tightfisted; Can His servants be less?

Hold fast the confidence and the rejoicing of the hope firm unto the end (Heb. 3:6 KJV).

Our Emotional God

God is neither a robot nor a despot without feeling. He made us in His image, and that means He has emotions as we have. His emotional side is revealed in what He likes and dislikes. "I will praise God's name in song and glorify him with thanksgiving. This will please the Lord more than an ox, more than a bull with its horns and hoofs" (Ps. 69:30-31). This verse says God can be pleased, and that He can be more pleased when we praise Him with our lips than when we write Him a large check.

Think of our sins. Is God pleased when we do wrong? Never! But He is pleased when we acknowledge our wrong and confess it. "You do not delight in sacrifice, or I would bring it.... The sacrifices of God are a broken spirit; a broken and contrite heart, O God, you will not despise" (Ps. 51:16-17). Confession is "Calvary action" because the suffering of Jesus makes the cross effective in us, and this really delights God. Sin is always destructive. God's anger against sin is not only because it hurts His holiness but it destroys us. So God is greatly pleased when we turn humbly to Him for cleansing and healing. He delights in reconciliation: "This brother of yours was dead and is alive again; he was lost and is found" (Luke 15:32).

God rejoices in reconciliation for then we become "normal" in His sight. We fulfill His original intent for us. Reconciliation gives Him pleasure because it means we accept what He has accepted, His values become ours, and we take on the flavor of Christ Himself. Jesus delights in the Father and the Father delights in the Son, both for the same reason, a shared nature. Therefore, the more like Jesus we become, the more we reflect His image back to God, and this fills Him with abounding pleasure.

How priceless is your unfailing love! Both high and low among men find refuge in the shadow of your wings. For with you is the fountain of life (Ps. 36:7,9).

Faith Blossoms in Uncertainty

Are you surrounded by a cloud of uncertainty? Take heart! "His purpose in the cloud is to simplify (purify) our belief" (Oswald Chambers). Faith, by its nature, must work in a world of uncertainty. In uncertainty faith is born and nurtured, and its mission is to destroy the uncertainty that surrounds our existence.

I think of Abraham. Everything about him was clouded with uncertainty. He obeyed God's call to go from Ur to Canaan "though he did not know where he was going" (Heb. 11:8). If Abraham had known he would not have needed faith. God always calls us to follow Him down unknown paths in order to give faith its reason for existence. His objective is to make us *believing* people.

God promised Abraham and Sarah a son, though it was evident that they were too old to have children. Yet God made the promise so that His purpose might stand through faith, not through the natural process. When Abraham's body was "as good as dead," there came descendants "as numerous as the stars" (v. 12). His faith triumphed over bodily weakness. So it was "by faith that Abraham... was enabled to become a father" (v. 11). Each passing year God's promise of a son seemed more unlikely until it reached the final stage of impossibility. Still Abraham trusted God. He believed that God could rejuvenate his body, overcome Sarah's age, and fulfill what He had sworn. So God did. Abraham's faith triumphed over daunting uncertainty which the failure of the natural process brings.

Still more, Abraham's faith battled the uncertainty of God's own promise. When the incredible word came that he must offer Isaac, the child of miracle, as a burnt offering on Mount Moriah, Abraham's faith could easily have crumbled. This was uncertainty at its worst. Mentally Abraham could not see how God could fulfill His promise through Isaac, yet ask for Isaac's death at the same time. Yet, "by faith Abraham, when God tested him, offered Isaac" (v. 17). God responded to faith, Isaac was spared, and Abraham's uncertainty vanished. Such is the triumph of simple faith in God!

Consider it pure joy . . . because you know that the testing of your faith develops perseverance (Jas. 1:2-3).

Living Above Disappointment

Jesus is not a "wrapped-in-cellophane" Savior. He took on Himself the common ills and burdens of humanity, especially the pain of disappointment.

How did He deal with it? Despite His powerful preaching/ healing ministry in the Decapolis area of Northern Galilee, the people turned against Him. He seemed to have failed; the people did not "repent" (Matt. 11:20). This in itself is revealing. Who ever heard more powerful preaching than that of Jesus? What generation has seen more miracles? What nation has been more favored than the people of whom Jesus was a part? And yet His kinspeople rejected Him. How deep and devious is the human heart!

Perfectly human, Jesus accepted this defeat and found solace in prayer. But his prayer was not the venting of His complaint, it was a gush of praise: "I praise you, Father... because you have hidden these things from the wise and learned and revealed them to little children. Yes, Father, for this was your good pleasure" (vv. 25-26). This praise was His confidence in the Father's will, the certainty of the goodness of the Father's purposes. He knew also that the Father made no mistakes. This was the Father's "good pleasure." Jesus, though the Son, was not coddled. "He learned obedience from what he suffered" (Heb. 5:8). From then on He would face increasing rejection until he arrived at the Father's destination for Him—Calvary. Even *this* was the Father's good pleasure.

Can we avoid disappointment? No more than Jesus could. But we can follow His path through disappointment until we find, as Jesus found, as the apostle Paul found, that God is beyond disappointment. Once we learn this priceless lesson, we will be able to live above disappointment. How fortunate we are to have a Savior who, by His example, enables us to see with crystal clarity the life that overcomes.

151

Delight yourself in the Lord and he will give you the desires of your heart. Commit your way to the Lord . . . and he will do this (Ps. 37:3-4).

What Does God Want Us For?

What does God want from us? Exactly the same as what He wanted from Jesus. This is a high, holy purpose indeed! And what an honor it implies!

God wants us for *pleasure*. Jesus fully satisfied His Father. "This is my Son, . . . with him I am well pleased" (Matt 3:17). God's pleasure in Jesus comes from His perfect representation of God in flesh. Seeing Jesus, we see the Father.

God wants us to afford Him the same pleasure. He saved us "in accordance with his pleasure and will" (Eph. 1:5). That was His initial purpose. Now He wants us to live like Jesus and so "please him in *every* way" (Col. 1:10a, emphasis added). How much like Jesus are we? If much, then we satisfy God's intention for us. Impossible? No! He *calls* us to it (2 Pet. 1:3).

God wants us for *fellowship*. John 17 describes the intrinsic relationship between Father and Son. The key to this relationship lies in the word "know." "Though the world does not know you, I know you" (v. 25). The world knows about God, Jesus knows Him. He talked about God from fresh, personal knowledge, as if He had always known Him, which He had. His knowledge was not book-learned or secondhand, but direct, personal, real.

God desires the same kind of fellowship with us. Salvation

itself is a fellowship: "[To] know you, the only true God" (v. 3). This fellowship begins at the cross; but once established, we are to keep "growing in the knowledge of God" (Col. 1:10b). Our knowledge of God must be firsthand. We can't book-learn or hand-copy our knowledge of God. We must, as Andrew Murray said, "Give God time to reveal Himself to us...to be quiet before Him...to receive the assurance of His presence." We must learn Him intimately by walking and talking with Him and doing His will.

You are a chosen people, a royal priesthood, a holy nation, a people belonging to God that you may declare the praises of him who called you out of darkness into his wonderful light (1 Pet. 2:9).

Called to Share the Glory of Christ

One of the privileges God has reserved for His children is to share the glory of His Son. "He called you to this through our gospel, that you might share in the glory of our Lord Jesus Christ" (2 Thess. 2:14). We may not understand fully what this means, but there are some glimmerings in the Word.

It means to share Jesus' *physical* glory. He promises that our body will be glorified like His. "[He] will transform our lowly bodies so that they will be like his glorious body" (Phil. 3:21). This means no more sickness, injury, handicap, or death. It is the triumph of the human body through the Savior, for we are, as L. E. Maxwell says, "Blood brothers with the King."

It means to share Jesus' *visible* glory. Jesus prayed, "Father, I want those you have given me to be with me where I am, and to see my glory" (John 17:24). This glory is now visible in heaven (Rev. 5). It will someday be visible on earth; "Every eye will see him" (1:7). And also *us*, since we are called to partake of the same glory. A pagan critic of early Christians said, "These wretched people have persuaded themselves... that they will live forever." Of course, Jesus promised we would—and gloriously!

It means to share Jesus' *regal* glory. When He returns He will not come alone. He will return with angels and saints (Matt. 24:30-31; Jude 14). The church will come as His bride, prepared in fine linen, clean and bright (Rev. 19:7-8). As His bride, we will share the regnant glory of Christ as He comes to establish righteousness on earth.

It means to share Jesus' *moral* glory. Of all glories, this one is the greatest. The others are in the future, but this one we can share now (1 Pet. 2:9). The glories of Jesus are moral glories— the purity of His life, the perfection of His qualities. The Holy Spirit now gradually changes us into His moral likeness (2 Cor. 3:18). "Christ lives in me" (Gal. 2:20) is not only a doctrine, but a reality, as Hudson Taylor discovered. Then he became not only a believer in Christ, but a revealer of Christ as well. What an adventure for this life, what a glorious destiny in the life yet to be!

God... conformed [us] to the likeness of his Son, that he might be the firstborn of many brothers (Rom. 8:29).

Finishing Well

The contemporaries of Jesus said of Him, "He has done everything well" (Mark 7:37). Indeed He did! Best of all, He *finished* well (John 19:30). God, who fashioned the universe from nothing, would not leave the task of redemption unfinished. He has the same purpose for us; He wants us to finish our pilgrimage well. The Spirit who empowered Jesus both to live and die well is the One who lives within us for the same purpose: to complete the Father's will in each of us *victoriously*.

David said, "It is God who arms me with strength and makes my way perfect" (Ps. 18:32). As with David, God's intention is to bring us to perfection! That is, He wants to complete in us the work He had chosen for us to do. He wants us to end as *victors*. In his seventieth year, Hudson Taylor said to his family, "I have just finished reading the Bible through, today, for the fortieth time in forty years." This remark seemed to symbolize the finishing of his earthly work, for shortly afterward, in Hunan, China, he was highly acclaimed by thousands of Chinese who called him their "Missionary Benefactor." It was there he died, finishing well.

Paul said, "He who began a good work in you will carry it on to completion" (Phil. 1:6). This is always the Father's aim—to complete things. Of his own work Paul said, "I have fought the good fight, I have finished the race, I have kept the faith" (2 Tim. 4:7). Not only did Paul finish well, he *knew* he did! Yes, I believe we can know we have finished our course and that we finished it well. Living closely to God and following carefully the pattern given to us by Jesus, we can know beforehand that our entrance into the everlasting kingdom will be abundant (2 Pet. 1:11). What greater joy is there than to realize we have contributed to the glory of God on this earth? What greater satisfaction than to hear the Father say, "Well done, faithful servant."

> If I still hold closely to Him, What hath He at last?
> Sorrow vanquished, labor ended, Jordan passed
> (John Mason Neale).

He said to me: "It is done. I am the Alpha and the Omega"
(Rev. 21:6).

"Behold, I Make All Things New"

God's dealings with His people always pass through phases. But no matter the phase, His aim is newness. "Behold, I make all things new!" (Rev. 21:5, KJV). Look at Israel. A long phase of their history was spent in Egypt (400 years), most of the time as slaves. It was a dark and bitter era, and the people cried out bitterly to God (Ex. 2:23). The Lord heard and delivered them by means of a lamb (Ex. 12). The lamb was sacrificed in the evening of the fourteenth day, and early the next morning the Israelites began their tedious trek to the promised land.

At Calvary, Jesus experienced death for us all. But it was temporary, as all God's phases are. The hour of "darkness" gave way to the early morning of triumphant resurrection. Rejoice, He is alive forevermore! A dawn has broken for us which will never cease. Once, when Billy Graham visited Bonn, Germany, Chancellor Konrad Adenauer asked him, "Do you believe that Jesus Christ is alive?" Graham replied, "Yes, sir, I do." Adenauer answered, "So do I. If Jesus Christ is not alive, then I see no hope for the world. It is the resurrection that gives me hope for the future."

Indeed, human history will end, first in a gathering darkness (1 Thess. 5:1-8), then in the full shining of glory at the coming of the Lord Jesus (Rev. 1:7). His return will mark the end of the old phase of human life and bring heaven's abundant newness to earth. Warfare will cease, and peace and justice will reign throughout the planet. This will be the final phase of God's great, eternal newness.

This final dawn will end our long warfare with sin. The horror of man's "dark ages" will dissolve, and God's people will gather to participate in the triumph of Christ. The voices of heaven and earth will join to rejoice.

In every land begin the song,
To every land the strains belong:
In cheerful sounds all voices raise,
And fill the world with loudest praise (Isaac Watts).

***Blessing and honor and glory and power Be to Him who sits
on the throne, And to the Lamb, forever and ever!
(Rev. 5:13, NKJV).***

Topical Index